THE CRYSTAL HEART

THE CRYSTAL -HEART-

A Practical Guide to Healing the Heart Centre with Crystals

RONALD LOUIS (RA) BONEWITZ

THE AQUARIAN PRESS

First published 1989

© Ra Bonewitz 1989

British Library Cataloguing in Publication Data

Bonewitz, Ra
The crystal heart : a practical guide to
healing the heart centre with crystals.
1. Man. Heart. Therapy. Alternative methods
I. Title
616.1'206

ISBN 0-85030-701-5

*The Aquarian Press is part of the Thorsons Publishing Group.
Wellingborough, Northamptonshire, NN8 2RQ, England.*

Printed and bound in Great Britain by
Mackays of Chatham PLC, Chatham, Kent

3 5 7 9 10 8 6 4

Acknowledgements

To Miles and Mary Tuely, for their invaluable support.

To Lilian: wherever your path may take you in this world or others, my love will walk with you always—part II!

Contents

Introduction

As many readers will know, I have been involved with crystals since I was 6 years old, when I began my first crystal collection. I was a self-taught lapidary by the age of 16, and went on to university to take a degree in geology.

My professional work has included gem-mining, studies of crystal chemistry (I did some early studies on the properties of ruby for lasers), and advanced studies in geochemistry, specializing in crystal chemistry. On a more esoteric level, I have been involved with crystals since 1977, when I found and cut a set of crystals for the Findhorn Community in Scotland. Through the intervening years, I have been very involved in the New Age movement, and have expanded my studies to include psychology and cosmology.

I have seen the crystal movement develop throughout the world over these past few years, and I have become increasingly uncomfortable with what I have been seeing. Crystals have begun to take on their own mythology, and I have watched thousands of people lead themselves into quite an extraordinary set of illusions about them. From a varying set of motivations, I see people being led further and further from their own purpose in being on the earth: to discover themselves, and to bring that discovery into full manifestation as a fully realized human being. To this end, much of what is being taught about crystals is worse than useless, it is a false path, and a distraction from the crystal user's true purpose in life.

Not that anyone's immortal souls are being swallowed up by them; no real harm is being done, but a great deal of time is being wasted. This is a time of major change on the earth. Forces are in action to bring the earth and its inhabitants back into alignment with the universe's own purpose. Not that we are being manipulated by some outside force; we are part of the essential Being of the universe, and it is our own inner connection to this Beingness that is personally and individually moving us toward greater alignment.

What I am presenting to you in this book is a very direct line to your own personal realization. If you are through playing games with your own life, then this book is for you.

I have designed this book to help you avoid many of the pitfalls in the self-realization process; I can do this, because I have fallen into a great many of them myself! Through this book I hope to demystify the entire process and help you get directly to your goal without a great deal of energy-wasting mumbo jumbo in the process.

Everything in this book works.

I do not pretend that this book is the final answer to your own self-discovery process; but you will find much in it that will supplement other inner processes, or stimulate them.

Those who are seeking an instant cure will find little of use here. Herewith I present you with one of the great non-secrets of the universe: Things Take Time. Many of the issues which you are resolving in yourself are lifetime lessons.

Be kind to yourself; give yourself Time.

I bless you on your journey.

RA BONEWITZ

1 The Heart of the Matter

According to an eastern story, when the gods decided to create the Universe, they created the stars, the sun, and the moon. They created mountains and seas and flowers, and clouds. Then they created human beings. And, finally, they created Truth.

Because the search for truth is the greatest adventure in the universe, the gods decided to hide truth, to prolong the search.

'Let's put Truth on top of the highest mountain', said one of the gods. Certainly it will be hard to find it there.'

'Let's put it on the farthest star,' said another.

'Let's hide it in the deepest and darkest of caves.'

'Let's conceal it on the dark side of the moon.'

At the end, the wisest and most ancient god said, 'No, we will hide Truth inside the heart of human beings. In this way they will look for it all over the Universe, without being aware of having it inside themselves all the time.'[1]

The process of opening or healing the heart, then, is not merely a process of 'repairing the damage'. The goal of working on the heart is not to make your life as it is to work better. It is not to fix things. There is nothing to fix.

Opening the heart is to seek Truth at its deepest and most profound level. And in finding that truth, what you will find is that you are already perfect exactly as you are: perfect, with all of your limitations. The purpose of limitation is its capacity to express distinction in order to express uniqueness. You are

[1] Quoted in *What We May Be*, by Piero Ferrucci.

who you uniquely are *because* of your limitations. If there were no limitations, everything would simply flow into everything else, and there would be no opportunity for unique self-expression. This was, of course, how the universe was in the beginning—an amorphous mass of energy, with no opportunity for self-discovery.

As your heart opens, as you begin to find and expose deeper and deeper levels of Truth, what will change is your *perspective*.

As you progress deeper and deeper into the opening process, you will find that you have less and less need to define your experience, and are more content to just let it be however it is. The need to define, to interpret, to analyse, all exist as one level of consciousness. The goal in opening the heart is to *shift your level of consciousness*. Or, perhaps a bit more accurately, to enable you to discover other levels of consciousness in yourself and to shift into those levels of consciousness at will, according to the appropriateness of the situation in which you find yourself.

Human beings exist at many levels, and in many consciousnesses. Because limitation is a necessary facet of living in matter, there will be some levels of consciousness that operate more efficiently in one set of situations, whereas other levels of consciousness will operate more efficiently in other situations.

This book about opening the heart is written around the use of crystals as a tool. By no means whatever do I mean to suggest that crystals are the *only* tool. They are just one among many, and they are intended to supplement whatever other methods and means you are using in your own opening process.

Nor are they some sort of magic key that will suddenly and abruptly open the door to enlightenment. The process of opening the heart is a process of gradual unfoldment, to find the jewel within, the jewel of Truth.

Nor is the Truth which we find, from our limited perspective before opening, that which we would expect it to be. One image of inner truth is the jewel in the centre of the lotus. At one level of seeing a jewel, it is a thing which is hard, fixed, and immutable.

And yet on another level, a jewel is composed of many facets, of many reflections, each one reflecting the constantly changing patterns of light and colour that are presented to it. At another level of seeing things, the truth is the same. It is constantly changing, as the world around it changes.

Thus may our inner truth reflect the constantly changing patterns of our own lives. Life is an adventure; it is an exploration of what is, and what may be. What your life will be in the future is only a reflection of what it is now, and the decisions and actions that you take *now*. Thus, it is constantly changing, and constantly shifting. A constant series of new reflections, reflecting from your own personal inner truth.

We live in a world of paradox. We live in a world of form, and yet the essential aspects of our own being are formless.

A paradox can never be resolved by trying to find exact definitions, to find final truths, ultimate answers. Until we let go of our need to control, to resolve, we will be in a constant state of crisis as we move closer and closer to our own inner paradox. These crises will express themselves in many ways: through disturbances of mind, through illnesses in the body, through stress and tension and breakdown. These are, on the whole, healthy processes, as long as we are prepared to use them as learning tools. The inward journey, the healing process, is one of balancing and harmonizing many seemingly opposing forces.

As one progresses inward, as one feels the impulse for change, there is often a feeling of urgency. In my own process of unfoldment, I was naive enough to believe that by focusing totally on myself, I could complete the process in a few months! Not that undertaking this process did me any harm; but it did serve to shatter the illusion of rapid change. I know now that change is an ongoing process, and that the goal, as I once viewed it, does not exist: to become such and such a person, or such and such a Being. There is no final goal to our becoming. There is no finished product.

But does this mean we should not begin the journey? If there is nowhere to go, what is the point in leaving in the first place?

If I were to slip back into my old thinking, and need to define a goal, I would now say that the goal is change. The living universe is a place of constant change; not to change is to stagnate. To stay frozen is, ultimately, to die. Sometimes it takes a dramatic event or realization to shatter us out of our mould. Otherwise, we keep travelling the same path, and just restating over and over and over again our old and limited beliefs of who we are. It is this necessity, therefore, that draws to us a state of crisis. Thus, opening the heart centre is a process of transformation, of change. It is to open ourselves to a whole new view of ourselves, not merely to polish up the old view so it looks even better.

As this process of inner seeking unfolds, there will be times beset with fear, with bewilderment and uncertainty. As the old and safe ways begin to dissolve, you will move into new ways of seeing things, new ways of doing things. And, because these are unfamiliar, they feel unsafe. And therefore, frightening. Above all, remember that it is safe to feel fear.

Let us now begin to look more directly at the heart centre, and what it represents.

We are all familiar enough with the heart as a mechanical device—a pump. If this were the only function of the heart, how simple it would all be! And yet, as a symbol, the pump is perhaps not inappropriate. For it is from the heart that all nourishment is circulated to all aspects of our physical being. The components may be created elsewhere, such as in the respiratory or digestive systems, but it is only through the unceasing effort of the heart to circulate the blood that all of the benefits of other parts of the body can be felt throughout.

Thus it is so at other levels. Although the benefits to our entire being may be generated elsewhere, even elsewhere in the universe, those benefits only come to us through the source of our heart.

It is significant to notice the amount of language that has grown up around the various functions of the heart as a source of Being. We use the expression 'to go to the heart of the matter' when we are talking about going to something in its pure essence; the heart, then, becomes a reflection of our own pure essence. It also means the deepest level of our being, as in the expression 'you have reached my heart', which means that we have reached the very soul. And the phrase 'with all my heart' means total commitment, as it comes from the very deepest level of our being.

We speak of a persons being open or closed, relative to the approaches of the world. We even see this in body language— puffing up the chest, or sticking out the chest is a gesture of defiance, indicating that our heart is closed. The gesture of moving one's shoulders forward, as one would do in reaching out with the arms, can be seen as an open-hearted gesture, of reaching out. Paradoxically, either of these two gestures frozen as a continuous body posture will usually mean just the opposite.

We also associate the feeling of love with the heart. 'To open your heart', means to be willing to take in the love of another person; 'giving your heart' means to fall in love. And, 'wearing your heart on your sleeve' means that you are openly looking for love.

The heart, then, is an organ associated with feeling. The heart expands with joy, or it has the feeling of shrinking with anxiety or disappointment. And a broken heart is a feeling associated with a great deal of anxiety, pain, or discomfort in the heart area. The word broken does not mean broken in two pieces—but rather a feeling that a connection has been broken.

Truly, the experience of opening the heart is of opening oneself to higher and higher levels of love. And I am speaking not of love on a personal or sensual level, although as one's heart opens those aspects of love also increase, but rather of achieving a higher energy state, and a basic well-being that radiates from the inner Source.

It is an outflowing from the inner Being that embraces the whole Being, and radiates outward from it to embrace everyone and everything that comes near. And it is not a conscious act of embracing; it just *is*.

It is a movement beyond the emotions; emotions are always a distortion of our deepest ability to love. Christ consciousness is often referred to as an ability for unconditional love. But what is the exact quality of that love? Jesus said that he also came to bring a sword.

When you recognize that what love really is, *is* the source of your being, and that all emotions are distortions of that, you create a force in your life that is like a sword—it will destroy the you who you thought you were, and out of those flames will emerge the real You.

In Figure 1 is shown the flow of energy from the Inner Being, the core of which is the heart. In Latin, *cor* means the heart.

The first channel of communication for the heart is through the throat and mouth. It is the newborn's first channel of expression as it reaches for the mother's breast with the lips and mouth. However, a baby doesn't reach with the lips and mouth alone; it also reaches with its heart.

In the kiss, we have retained our awareness of this movement as an expression of love. But, a kiss may be a gesture of love, or an expression of love; the difference is whether one's

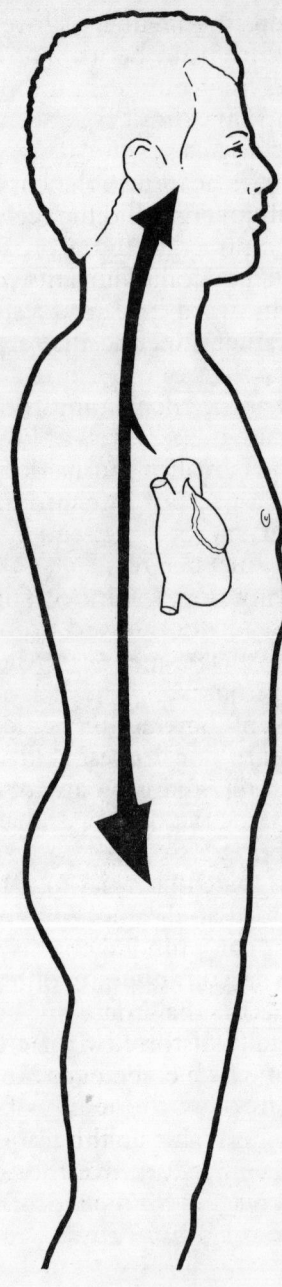

Figure 1

heart is in it or not, and that depends on whether the channel
of communication from the heart is open.

The second channel for the heart is through the arms and
hands as they reach out to touch. Here too the action can be
an expression of love, or a gesture, depending on whether the
feeling flows from the heart into the hands. Loving hands are
highly charged with energy, and have a healing quality in the
touch.

The third channel of communication of the heart is downward through the waist and pelvis, to the genitals. Sex is an
act of love, but once again, it can simply be a gesture, or a
true expression of love if one's heart is really in it. If the feeling of love for one's partner is strong the sexual experience
has an intensity that makes the orgasm an ecstatic event. In
such a case, one can actually feel one's heart leap for joy at the
moment of climax.

So, as the heart heals, becomes more open, all of the functions of human life become richer and fuller. If one wants to
live fully and richly, it is *only* possible if one opens one's heart
to life and to love. Without love—for one's self, for one's fellow
human beings, for nature and for the universe, a person is
cold, detached and inhuman. The lack of this love, that is an
open-hearted connection with everything that surrounds us,
leaves us with a sense of alienation, and separation from the
flow of life around us. That is because the flow of life *within*
us is blocked, and the world around us merely reflects that
fact to us.

In Figure 2, we see an impulse coming outward from the
heart centre through the various layers that surround the
heart. We can see that a blockage in any of those layers will
cause a distortion in the flow of energy, so that by the time
the love impulse reaches the surface, the personality expression,
it can become totally distorted. If the blockages are severe
enough, by the time love emerges at the surface, it can come
out as hate! In many of us, the energy of love working its way
outward from our heart through the blockage has become so
painful that we disassociate ourselves from it—in other words,
the mind and the body have become separate. In this situation,
we say that the head rules the heart.

It is the final betrayal of our own hearts.

In Figure 2, we can see that the individual represented by
the diagram has experienced a great deal of anxiety, and has
developed a series of defences to protect his heart. The heart

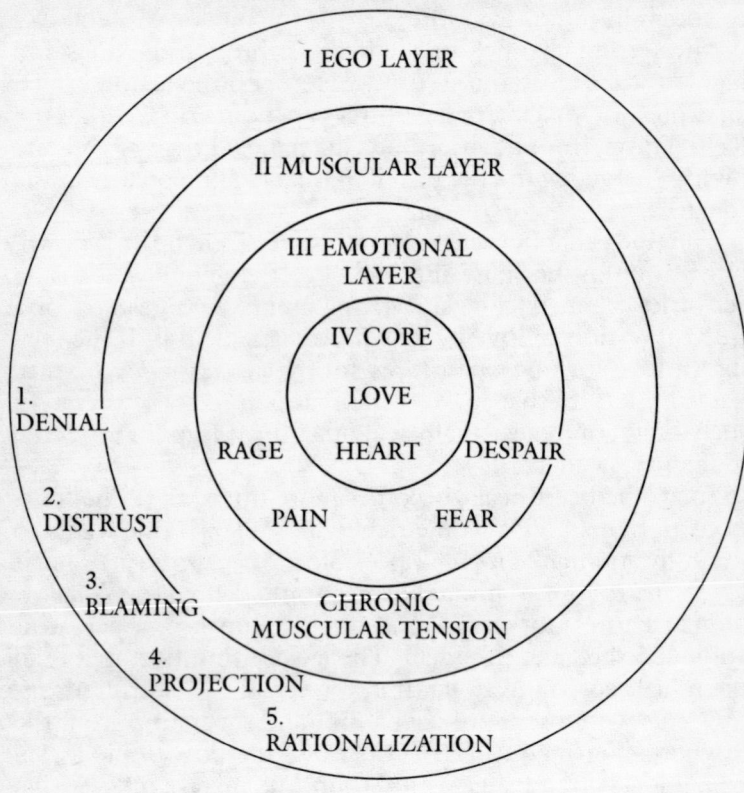

Figure 2

is the most sensitive organ of the body, and any interrupting of its rhythm of function, either physically or psychically, is a terrifying experience. In order to protect ourselves from this terror, we erect defences. These become powerful barriers, and are the blockages that must be worked through in later life to realize the full re-awakening of our heart-self.

The layers are as follows:

a) Denial
b) Distrust
c) Blaming
d) Projection
e) Rationalizations and intellectualizations.

In the muscular layer, we find the chronic muscular tensions that support the ego defences and at the same time protect

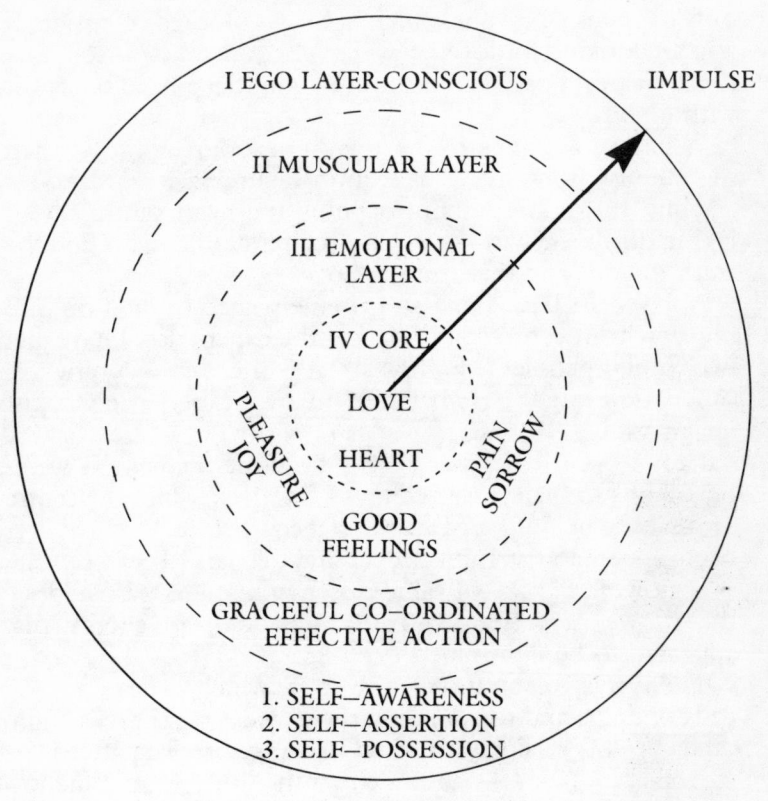

Figure 3

the person against the underlying suppressed feelings in the emotional layer, that he dares not express.

In the emotional layer, we find the suppressed feelings of rage, panic, terror, despair, sadness, and pain. These are all of the feelings that felt threatening to the heart, and thus have become suppressed.

Finally, in the very deepest level of our Being, is the core or heart, from which the feeling to love and be loved derives.[2]

The deepest core of our being, then, where our soul resides, *is* love, and is our own source of love. One of the most difficult realizations is that we are our own source of love—that it does not come from outside. No one can give it to us. And yet, we desperately seek some perfect partner who

[2] Alexander Lowen, *Bioenergetics*, p. 119.

will give us all of the love we deeply desire for ourselves. This only happens when our source of love is blocked off inside. If you are looking for love anywhere else, outside yourself, that is the clearest possible reflection of your deep need to seek it within you.

When we are open to our own inner source of love, then the impulse flows freely, as seen in Figure 3.

Thus, this book is about opening the heart centre, about taking down the barriers to your own inner flow. To find the truth in you; and that truth is Love.

A few years back I had an extremely deep meditation into my own heart centre. Since having the experience, I have met two other people who had exactly the same experience, otherwise I might have believed my own experience was just imagination.

I can't even remember exactly how the meditation went, but all of a sudden I realized that I was deeper into the centre of my own being than I had ever been before (or have ever been since), and as I got deeper and deeper, I became aware of a glowing light. As I came closer to that light, I could see that it was a pattern; a pattern made from energy that appeared to be light blue in colour.

There was a central structure to it, which appeared to be rods of light, and surrounding those rods of light were hundreds of dots of light, arranged in a very precise pattern.

In that moment, I was aware that the 'rods' were somehow the core of the structure, and that each of the blue dots was an experience. I knew that I was literally looking at the centre of my own being.

I knew that who I was as a being was an accumulation of all my experiences, and that those experiences were all linked together in a pattern that looked very much like the inner structure of a crystal! I do not in any way mean to imply that it *was* a crystal, but only that there was a very precise structure made up of energy.

On the other hand, I am absolutely certain that when we use crystals as reflections of the inner Being, this is precisely what we are reflecting—our own inner patterns. This is also why when we choose a crystal instinctively, when we go by our 'feels right' feeling, what we are really doing is tuning into our own heart centre, to the very depth of our own being, and seeing an outworking of the universal law 'Like recognizes Like'.

It was my realization that the world around us is really a world of reflections, that led to my own inner realization of the importance of crystals as tools of self-healing. Self-healing in the truest sense of the word—healing the Soul.

Something I have always noticed with children is they are instinctively attracted to crystals. Every time I have had a display of crystals at an exhibition, almost every child that goes past will be drawn like a magnet. And whose inner being is more open, is more attuned to the world around them, than a child's?

I was involved in a series of experiments a few years ago that lent direct evidence to the idea that, at a very deep level, the human body is intuitively responsive to crystals. We were using a device called a Mind Mirror, a device which measures the brainwave output at a number of different levels, from the totally conscious, to the totally unconscious. Besides recording the output, the brainwave pattern is also displayed in rows of coloured lights, on a board divided to display left and right hemispheres of the brain. Originally designed as a biofeedback device, it is possible to see very accurately the balance between the left and right hemispheres in the brain, and the patterns of brainwave output as you perform various tasks (thinking, meditating, etc).

We had no idea what sort of responses, if any, we would see on the machine when crystals were placed near the body. In the experiment we finally designed, the subject was blindfolded, and his ears were plugged to eliminate as much outside noise as possible. We decided to use a crystal passed through the chakra points, as it was suspected that we would see the maximum body response, if any, when crystals were passed through these energy centres.

The crystals we were using (quartz, tourmaline and topaz) were then taped to the end of a metre stick, so that the experimenter's hand was nowhere near the body, thus reducing the likelihood of any input from his own energy. The subject then entered a state of meditation (the subject chosen was one who had a good balance between left and right brain), and the crystals were passed through the chakra points along the subject's back. This was done to ensure that there were the minimum possible audio and visual cues to the subject when the crystals were actually near his body. They were passed at distances from about an inch, out to a foot.

In every single instance, when any of the crystals were passed through the lower three chakras, there was an instantaneous flare of brainwave activity in the delta and theta levels of activity, levels that go from unconscious to subconscious. This happened with each type of crystal, and at each distance out to a foot beyond the body. We were not concerned with distance from the body at that particular time, so there may well have been activity beyond a foot from the body, but it was not checked.

We felt it significant that the chakras below the heart, those most directly connected to the energies of the earth, were those most strongly affected.

This was not intended to be a definitive experiment, but I believe that it underlines certain of the points I will make throughout this book—that there is some intuiting mechanism in the human being, and especially in the human body, that recognizes and responds to the presence of crystals. I believe that we can say this is a piece of direct proof of the universal law 'Like attracts (recognizes) Like'.

We are seeing the inner recognition mechanism at work and realize it is this mechanism that is responsible for the 'miraculous healings' that appear to take place using crystals. This can certainly give the *appearance* that crystals are some-how emitting healing rays. I am certain that what we are seeing activated is the body's own mechanism for healing, as if we were holding up a mirror of perfection, and the body is responding saying, 'yes, that's how I really want to be!'

We know from recent studies of the brain that only about one trillionth of the information reaching the brain ever gets to the conscious mind, therefore we are totally unaware of almost everything that goes on in our minds. Would it be any surprise that the mechanisms of healing, of intuition, of inner recognition, are not processes of which we are fully conscious?

Your Inner Being, the real You, has only one goal—self-completion. To this end, your Inner Being will use whatever is necessary to complete itself—including making you ill, if you refuse to see any of the other reflections of self-knowing in the world around you. Likewise, the Inner Being will draw you very strongly to any mirroring situation that will lead you to greater depths of self-discovery.

Because of the correspondence between your inner pattern and the inner patterns of crystals, is it any wonder that the Inner Being will draw you so strongly to crystals? At a very profound level, they are perfect mirrors of the self!

2   A Matter of the Heart

Dr John Harrison states quite clearly: 'Disease is both self created and self cured.'

He further emphasizes the point that this concept is very hopeful for the patient. As we become more and more familiar with our investment in developing diseases, we can begin to assume more and more control over our disease, and over our personal destiny. He also states:

> Illness is the physical and psychological result of unresolved needs, not a malfunction of a machine caused by unknown or external factors. *The client is needy, rather than sick, and has exercised an honourable option to him to take care of himself as best he can.*[1] (Emphasis in original)

He underlines very clearly my own philosophy: that to remove the symptoms creates no healing whatever. Unless the underlying psychological causes are discovered and dealt with, the disease process will simply repeat itself somewhere else. The ultimate outcome of discovering why we have given ourself a particular disease, comes from discovering what need in ourself was being unfulfilled. And as we do so, we can choose: to continue with our disease, as it does serve a useful purpose in meeting our needs, or to choose to meet that need in a healthier, possibly more self-serving way.

Dr Moss relates the disease process to various levels of energy; human beings exist at many levels.

At the lowest energy level, are the diseases that are clearly separate entities—viruses, bacteria, etc. These are easily

[1] John Harrison, *Love Your Disease*, p. 4.

distinguishable from our own body, and *cause* malfunctions of the body, rather than *are* malfunctions of the body.

High energy diseases are those which are direct malfunctions of the body—cancer, heart disease, any disease which is a direct cellular breakdown as opposed to an invasion of the body by outside organisms.

He likens the understanding of these two types of disease processes to Newtonian and Einsteinian physics. Newton had a basic and thorough understanding of the physics of slow moving, low energy bodies such as planets and comets. But applying the same ideas to atoms required a total shift of our understanding of the nature of physical reality. It wasn't until Einstein formulated basic relations between matter and energy, concepts that were totally unsuspected in Newton's day, that we were able to understand the workings of high-energy levels of being—particles, atoms, and energy itself.

The perpetual change we are now undergoing is to understand that the human body exists at many levels, and that some of these levels are totally energetic in nature (often referred to as the Subtle bodies in alternative practice).

The high energy diseases occur when we make choices that are not in harmony with our own highest energy level—the soul level of our existence; they come from unresolved, deep-level conflict between our *ideas* about living, and our own deeper *experience* of living.

But to simply be told that these conflicts exist does not resolve them; the only way we can resolve them is to directly experience them. And to directly experience them we need to make a perceptual shift in ourselves, a shift that enables us to directly perceive and experience those conflicts, and thereby resolve them and release them.

Cancer in particular is one of these high energy diseases, indicating an extremely deep level of inner conflict, creating enormous stress at the cellular level, which, when combined with the numerous toxins available in our environment, produce cancerous cells.

Yet we are so used to this inner conflict, indeed, we may have been living with it since infancy, that we do not perceive it because of its familiarity. Moss likens this to the city-dweller who is oblivious to the rumble of traffic around him—it is not until we are able to step outside that environment, to shift our perception, that we are able to notice it. In this example perhaps a few weeks in the quiet countryside releasing our inner tensions and attuning ourselves to the tranquility of nature will create that perceptional shift whereby we wonder how we ever lived with all the noise of the city. But, were you never to leave the city, it would be very difficult for you to directly perceive the amount of background noise that exists, because of its familiarity.

The exercises in this book are specifically designed to create the sort of perceptual shifts that are necessary to be able to start resolving those inner conflicts in your Being. The good news here is that because of their high energy, shifts in perception (healing) can take place very rapidly as you shift into higher levels of awareness. The intuitive recognition that takes place at a cellular level in the presence of crystals is a direct inner experience of one of these perceptual shifts, and, as mentioned earlier, probably accounts for the apparent 'miraculous' healing that takes place with crystals. I am also reminded here of a comparison between the mineral kingdom and the human personality—a mineral is soft and flexible when its energy bonds are fairly weak, in other words, in a condition of low energy. In minerals that are hard and brittle and easily broken, there is a very high energy bond which, although it gives a great deal of rigidity, also makes it very subject to breakage. Doesn't this sound a bit like certain personality types: a flexible personality type, who is able to 'bend with the wind', and is therefore subject perhaps to lower energy disease, if to any disease at all; and the very rigid type of personality, very locked up in its own energy and beliefs, and therefore easily broken—subject to very high energy diseases such as cancer. Psychological research has shown this to be exactly true: that the extremely rigid personality types, highly locked up emotionally, and highly inflexible, are extremely high cancer risks. These types of individuals are also very locked up in the heart centre, and, once again, the incidence of heart disease is astronomical.

Dr Moss says about the development of cancers:

> We would like to continue believing that the human immune system . . . has all of a sudden stopped functioning, and allowed the development of the tumour. . . . In fact, the human immune system may *not* be failing. Perhaps it is simply not subtle enough to recognize the force it is dealing with.[2]

[2] Richard Moss, M.D., *The I that is We*, p. 57.

Our diseases, especially high energy diseases like cancer and heart disease, therefore become open doors, open invitations to us to shift our levels of awareness, but to shift them into levels which ultimately serve not only to heal our disease, but to open our inner awareness to more subtle levels of ourselves, to resolve the conflicts that keep us away from our true inner Source. This is certainly the experience of numerous participants in self-development courses that I have been involved with—as deeper and deeper levels of Self awareness occur, cancers tend to disappear.

And for 'healers', the old adage 'physician, heal thyself', is never more true.

This doesn't mean we have to become 'perfect' to do any good work in the world; but we have to just keep working on it. The law of synchronicity (the law that when an event is right all other events are synchronized around it), will see to it that anyone we attract to ourselves in a 'healing' situation will have something in themselves that we've already taken care of in ourselves, and therefore we can help reflect back to them their own need for change.

The subject of self-healing, especially of the heart, is what this book is about.

If healing is really sorting out our inner beliefs, then self-healing ultimately can be only one thing—self-discovery.

Now for some of us that's not very good news, because it makes us look inward, rather than outward. It makes us look at ourselves. That's the thing most of us have the greatest fear of doing, and it's not easy. It's not *supposed* to be easy. Earth is a hard school. It's a university, not a kindergarten, and if you as a Being weren't ready for the hard course, you wouldn't be on the earth in the first place.

In my own experience of self-discovery at first I rather dreaded the process. I thought: What will I find when I really get in there? Am I really the never-good-enough person I came out of my childhood believing myself to be?

By the way, parents *all* fail: every parent fails; no child ever gets enough parenting. It is *necessary* for us to fail as parents, and for your parents to have failed, because if they hadn't we'd have nothing to learn. In our early childhood environment our parents set up for us our learning experiences.

I have been in geology for many years, doing a lot of collecting and mining of crystals and gems. I've done a lot of exploring in 'outback' sort of places, and to me it's always been a fascination to be in a place where very few people, if any, have ever been before; to walk over the next hill and see what's there, and maybe the first human being for a thousand years to look over a particular scene. Once I got through the initial fears of what I was going to find, I managed to transfer that same excitement of discovery to finding myself. I found things in me that have been, in my way of thinking about myself originally, every bit as alien as the new landscapes unfolding in front of me. And as I discovered them, every bit as fascinating. Also as I let go of some of the barriers and the blocks inside, my body has changed.

Since I started my own intensive inner-development, inner-discovery process, I have lost nearly 30 pounds in weight without dieting—I've lost weight on junk food! My body shape has changed, the shape of my face has changed: my body is physically a different body than the body that I had two years before this process began. Also I've been healthier, and my vitality and quality of aliveness have improved. Just from self-discovery!

What I have found in my experience is that crystals are wonderful mirrors, mirrors of the Self. Remember that crystals are very subtle energy patterns; they are the basic patterns of creation, and those patterns are a part of you. They are part of who you are, who you've always been and who you always will be.

We have physical mirrors to look at our physical bodies and see how things are progressing; we have a physical body that makes itself ill when it's trying to tell us we need to look at our beliefs. And now we have crystals that can mirror to us the most fundamental, most 'divine' levels of ourselves. So we have a number of tools to get to grips with who we really are. I promise none of you will be disappointed when you find out. Quite the opposite. You are going to be overjoyed.

I know the blue light pattern in the heart that I described in Chapter 1 was my own soul, my own deepest inner being. What I've realized since is that when we use crystals for mirroring ourselves what we are really mirroring are our own deepest inner patterns.

There is a resonance between the crystal and that part of ourselves, so when we choose a crystal, instinctively we choose a crystal that vibrates in harmony with who we are. Therefore we have not just any old mirror of ourselves, but a very personal mirror which may not be a mirror for anyone else. Something about the make-up of that particular crystal will resonate with who you are.

On the subject of healing, I'd like to make it very clear that I am not in any way against the idea of 'healing' as it's normally thought of—as one person applying energy to another person.

As long as we're clear about what's happening; and what's happening is not that one person is 'making' another person 'better'. The old way of thinking is still in place very much in alternative practice, and it's the same philosophy that doctors have: There is something wrong with you, and I can make you better.

That isn't how it works. In fact, what's 'wrong' with the person in the conventional way of thinking, is in fact very much *right*. Illness is not something wrong with you. ILLNESS IS SOMETHING THAT YOUR BODY IS TRYING TO TELL YOU TO HELP YOU GET RIGHT. Illness is something that's trying to heal you at a very profound level. Illness is *healing*. Illness is about *healing the soul*, it's about healing the real you. So illness is a gift that you give to yourself in order to help yourself become whole and at one with the universe again. There's no one who can fix you except *you*.

A healer in the conventional sense can certainly help you in that process; every human being is a healer. Every human being has the capacity to help other human beings find that point of wholeness within themselves. Remember, this often takes place on a subtle level, and the interaction between the patient and the healer mostly takes place on a subconscious level. So at some subconscious level the person who is the 'healer' sets up a resonance with the person who is seeking to become whole within themselves, and, at a very subtle level, something shifts. But it's not as if the healer is 'making' the other person well. Until the 'patient' is prepared at some level or other to make an inner adjustment, nothing can happen. Even *God* can't heal a human being who doesn't want to be healed; and many of us have a lot of subconscious reasons for staying ill. In fact, from a psychological survival standpoint, perfectly good reasons for staying ill. But those reasons no longer serve us when we decide to start shifting within ourselves—to start becoming whole, harmonious, becoming one with creation around us.

One of the most powerful self-healing mechanisms is our

own heart. Our own heart has the power to transmute and shift our inner perceptions.

Dr Richard Moss reports an experience in dealing with a patient of his that clearly illustrates this power of transmutation.

He was interviewing a woman patient who was describing the painful death of her son. The other people in the room felt a growing sense of pathos, and as the woman proceeded with her story, she began to experience the terrifying fantasy of her son's death. She began to cry, her voice became broken and tremulous, and her respiration erratic. Dr Moss said, 'Allow the energy in your guts to lift into your chest.'

> Instantly, as if by magic, her voice became strong and clear, her breathing regular, and she cried out 'I did it!' She said, 'Just as you told me to lift the energy, I remembered what you had said about listening from an unconditional space while you were interviewing. The moment I remembered I felt the energy lift to my heart and I was free.'[3]

Dr Moss goes on to say:

> Unconditional love is the embracing of all experience and the bringing of all varying intensities to the level of the heart. At the heart level, unconditional love, which is an alive, vibrant, valueless state of awareness, replaces the varying intensities of mood and uncontrolled emotion and lifts the energy of these states into finer, more radiant quality.[4]

Unconditional love, then, is a tool of transformation. It is a way of shifting our level of experience. This in no way means to imply that it is *better* than other types of experience, but it is merely a window for seeing those other experiences in another way.

There is an old Chinese story that says:

> Before man becomes enlightened, he wakes up in the morning, goes out and works his fields, comes home in the evening, makes love to his wife, and goes to sleep.
>
> After a man becomes enlightened, he gets up in the morning, goes out and works his fields, comes home in the evening, makes love to his wife, and goes to sleep.

[3] Ibid., p. 23.
[4] Ibid., p. 22.

This story underlines the point I am trying to make here;
that the activities and experiences of your daily life may not
change one iota as you become more and more self-aware—
however, our *perception* of them may change dramatically. As
you shift the quality of the underlying energy, the *nature* of
the experience changes, even though the experience *itself* may
not change.

Unless you are coming from the heart, though, to quote
Dr Moss once again: 'Without unconditional love as the centre
. . . the ability to shift and transmute energies can become
just another manipulation of our ego power.'

This is not to say that you must go out and seek unconditional love: *it already exists inside you*. It is the most profound level of our Being. The process then is not to find it or
create it; the process is to uncover it.

Through the following exercises, you will have an opportunity to begin experiencing deeper and deeper levels of love
radiating from the centre of your own being. During these
exercises, it is desirable for you to experience physical sensations in the area of the heart. You may have great feelings of
radiating warmth, feelings of softness, feelings of melting.
And indeed, you may also experience physical pain. Should
you do so, there is no need for alarm. The psychological and
energetic armouring that has covered our heart is held in
place by severe muscular tension in the chest area. As we
begin to let go of the energetic armoury, those muscles will
begin to relax. It is rather like the experience of setting down
a heavy load that you have been carrying for longer than you
wished—when you finally put it down, you notice how tight
and cramped the muscles are.

**This does not in any way suggest that you should not
seek competent medical advice should you feel any sense
of discomfort or alarm about any of the physical sensations
that occur in any exercises throughout the book.**

Throughout the remainder of this book you will find a
number of exercises involving the use of crystals, leading you
through various avenues of self-exploration. These are all
exercises and techniques that I have used personally, and that
others have used with success also. It is not intended that
these exercises and processes will be the final answer in your
self-discovery process. *Life* is the teacher; *life* is the course. All
any course or technique or process can do is give you new
tools for looking at your own life, and what you have

attracted to yourself, in a different perspective.

I suggest that you read through each exercise and, if possible, put them on tape. You can then play them back to yourself as you do the actual exercise, leaving yourself enough time between the instructions to complete whatever images or processes are being suggested.

Some of these exercises are intended to invoke strong emotional responses. They may or may not do so, depending on how in touch you already are with your feelings, and whether or not you have done similar processes or exercises in the past.

If strong feelings do arise, express them. Feelings held in are of no value, and they are truly the blockages to who you really are.

Whether it is through the use of exercises and techniques in this book, through courses you may take or therapies you may undertake, you will find that as shifts begin to take place on the inner plane your life around you will begin to change also.

The opening and developing process often involves deep feelings coming to the surface, and it is important that you give yourself permission to express them in a safe and appropriate manner. Anger can be released by kicking on a bed or striking a pillow as in the supplementary techniques; sadness and grief by just giving yourself permission to cry. And overwhelming feelings that require a good scream to be released can be done in a car with the window closed, by parking somewhere away from where you will be overheard, or by doing it somewhere in traffic, where the traffic noise will cover your scream. There are many other techniques for working directly with your body, and I strongly recommend those from bioenergetics.

The bottom line for much of the work you will be doing with yourself will be about facing your own fears. There is only one way, ultimately, to deal with fear—sit there and feel it. A fear that is felt, that is confronted, will eventually fade away. Always remember that it is *safe to feel fear*.

During some of the processes in this book, there may be times when you will feel a great deal of personal distress, your body may be distinctly uncomfortable, or you may feel a great deal of confusion. I highly recommend that while you are involved in these processes you seek the guidance of a qualified counsellor or therapist, to aid you in your own growth and development. It is important to emphasize that *there is no technique, therapy, or developmental path that is right for everyone*.

This book presents you with a variety of techniques from a number of different aspects of self-discovery and self-development, but in no way is it all conclusive. You will undoubtedly find that you will wish to supplement the contents of this book from other sources, and I suggest you begin with the reading list at the end of this book. The opening of the Self is a multi-faceted operation, and many, many therapies and techniques may ultimately be used. I suggest that you keep a detailed notebook with the results of all of the various exercises in this book, and also keep a record of dreams or other life experiences that occur during the time you are using these techniques. Remember that life is the teacher; and all of the therapies and techniques you do with yourself are merely ways of living your life more fully and completely, and absorbing its lessons more fully.

In noticing the rhythms of your own body, I also suggest that you include in your notebook a daily record of your sleep state—how well you slept on any particular night and for how many hours. In doing this over a period of time, you will find certain natural rhythms that develop. Also note whether on any particular night you have been up beyond your usual time, such as at a party, and notice how over a period of time your rhythms are affected by this.

Also, in doing the various exercises in this book, I suggest that you do them in a place where it is appropriate to release emotional feelings. And keep a box of tissues at hand! Tears are the natural safety valve of the body, and are the safest form of emotional release.

If you are doing these exercises in the company of another person, or doing them with someone else, it is best that the other person does not interfere in your processes—if you are in the middle of a strong crying release, it will often disrupt the flow of your release for them to press tissues on you, or attempt to comfort you. It is important to realize that we discharge our unfelt feelings by *feeling* them, and any attempt to soothe them before they have been fully expressed is robbing you of your experience. As you do these various processes, you will discover that your own sense of appropriateness will guide you as to when you need aid from another person.

Always be aware of your own limits. If you are going into a

state where you feel uncertain of your ability to deal with any feelings that arise, then simply come out of the experience. This is not to imply, by the way, that all of the experiences in this book are in any way emotional or traumatic. Many of them will fill you with joy and excitement of new discovery of who you really are. *I suggest that you read the book through entirely before beginning any of the exercises.* Then you will have an overall picture of what is ahead, and can see the relevance of the various exercises as they occur. Don't be daunted by the task ahead—personal growth and development is a life-long process, and anyone who promises you an 'instant fix' is lying to you: it just doesn't happen that way. Crystals are no more capable of creating instant shifts than any other life process; they are not in any way 'magic pills'. And they certainly will not give you instant enlightenment. But, as you shall soon discover, they can be vitally important tools in your own self-discovery and self-healing process.

3   The Heart of Matter

Before we begin the Heart opening exercises it is necessary to look at the tools we will be using—crystals.

In the past few years there has been an enormous amount of information generated about crystals, through books and publications. Much of it, unfortunately, is total nonsense.

Not that the writers of these books and articles are deliberately attempting to mislead anyone—what they are writing and teaching comes from their own lack of critical examination of their subject.

In book after book, and article after article, the same myths about crystals are being repeated. If you look at the bibliography of most crystal books, you will find that for the most part, they are quoting other crystal books!

In this chapter we will look at some of the most common myths about crystals and gain a clearer understanding of what they will and won't do. Because we are using them as tools to gain access to the very clearest and purest part of ourselves, it is essential that we are not carrying a lot of misconceptions about them into our work with ourselves.

Crystals are forming all the time in the earth—perhaps beneath your own feet as you read these words.

The earth, which I view as a living being, is constantly renewing and regenerating its own crystal body. Just to give a bit of perspective on the earth, although we think of the earth as fairly solid and rigid, it is really in constant motion. The continents are moving about, mountains are being thrust up or eroded down, bits of continents are being pulled under to be remelted and returned to the surface as volcanoes and so forth. If we could stand back from the earth and compress time to where a million years would pass in a minute, we would see that the earth never stands still. The energy for all this movement is generated by the decay of radioactive elements deep in the interior of the earth which works its way outward as heat.

If we were to make a model of the earth the size of a football, and scale down the strength of the earth to the same scale, our football-size earth would be made of toothpaste!

The earth is arranged in three major layers—the core, mantle and crust. The core is made of very dense material, probably iron and nickel, and makes up a third of the diameter of the earth. The mantle, made of dense minerals of aluminium, iron, magnesium, silicon and oxygen, makes up almost the remaining two-thirds of the earth.

The crust, forming a very thin shell on the outside (about the thickness of a postage stamp on our football-sized toothpaste earth), is mostly made up of lighter minerals.

We will return to this structure of the earth shortly, as there are certain misconceptions about crystals and minerals that are directly connected to it. First, however, let's look at the definitions of the words 'mineral' and 'crystal'.

A **mineral** is a chemical substance which is part of the earth, and is not generated by some biological process. So, the name of any particular mineral is nothing more than the name of that particular chemical when it occurs as part of the earth.

For example, when aluminium and oxygen combine in the earth as a mineral, it is called corundum. When silicon and oxygen are combined in the earth, that chemical is called quartz. When sulphur and iron are combined in the earth, that chemical is called pyrite (or fool's gold). Every time we have a different chemical composition, it has a different name. So, if we add a bit of water to the silicon and oxygen mentioned previously, it is no longer quartz: it is now called opal. There are approximately 2,500 different minerals, each of which is chemically distinct from all the others.

A **crystal** is a mineral whose atoms have arranged themselves in very precise patterns, and, as a result of those precise patterns, occur in geometric forms, such as cubes, octahedrons, etc.

As we can see, crystals are rather special conditions of minerals. Only a very small percentage of any particular mineral will actually manifest as crystals. For example, perhaps only 1,000th of 1 per cent of quartz will be found as crystals—the remainder will just be whitish lumps. Likewise, a similar percentage of pyrite might be found as distinct crystals—the remainder is just brassy-looking lumps.

There is another state in which minerals are found—the state called **crystalline**. In this state, the patterns of atoms have formed as in crystals, but there has been no opportunity for the geometric forms to develop.

All crystals are formed from solutions—that is, something solid dissolved in something liquid. The liquid may be very fluid water carrying dissolved minerals coursing through cracks in other rocks, or it may be very thick and viscous magma, the consistency of putty. In either case, to varying degrees the atoms are free to move about and attach themselves in patterns that are consistent with their atomic attractiveness for one another.

At certain temperatures and pressures several atoms may be attracted to one another and yet other atoms will have no interest in them whatever. The other atoms, however, will be attracted to one another, and they will begin to form yet another mineral at exactly the same time and place. This is why several minerals can form simultaneously, such as the mineral feldspar, the mineral quartz, and the mineral mica, the three main constituents of the rock granite. They form more or less simultaneously, and because they are forming simultaneously tend to grow into one another, forming interlocking grains. Each has formed its own inner pattern, but, because there was no space available for faces to develop, no crystals have formed. The mineral grains which make up granite, then, are crystalline.

In other instances, where liquid is flowing through some sort of hollow space, usually a fracture in pre-existing rocks, there is open space and therefore an opportunity for flat faces, and the geometric forms begin to develop. Unless the crack (called a vein) fills itself up entirely with mineral matter, there will be a hollow where crystals have formed. The majority of crystals that we will be using as tools have formed in this manner.

Let me just briefly mention another use of the word 'crystal', because there is a tremendous amount of confusion about this word. The word is often applied to a type of glass. Now the word 'glass' is actually a very specific scientific word which has a very precise meaning. Glass is a liquid that is so solid it won't flow at ordinary temperatures. So window glass is actually a liquid; it is just very thick at normal temperatures. I met a glazier in Australia who told me that in removing glass from very old buildings, it was actually possible to measure the difference in thickness between the top and bottom of the pane—there had been that much flow over a century or so. The characteristic of a liquid is that its atoms are arranged in *no patterns whatever*; it's totally structureless. So to use the word 'crystal', which means totally and very precisely structured, and the word 'glass', which means absolutely no structure, means we use words that have absolutely opposite meanings.

If you had a bowl made of 'crystal' in the year 1300, it was made from a piece of quartz crystal. If you had anything made from 'crystal' before that time, it was made from quartz. When very colourless glass was made, glass that was as colourless as natural crystal became called 'crystal glass' to differentiate it from ordinary glass. In order to differentiate the natural stone, then, it became called 'rock crystal', as opposed to 'glass crystal' or 'crystal glass'. These names came into common use around AD 1500–1600.

So, let us go on to some of the myths and realities about crystals.

There is an astronomical amount of mythology growing up around the mineral quartz at the moment, all of it based on some fairly basic misunderstandings of the nature of the mineral kingdom.

The major myth about quartz is that it is somehow *special*. This specialness is a result of a number of misunderstandings, in particular the erroneous belief that quartz is the most abundant mineral in the earth. Not by a million miles.

If we are looking at the earth as a whole, the mantle makes up two-thirds of the earth, therefore we would expect that any mineral prominent in the mantle would be a likely candidate to be the most abundant. And this is exactly true.

There is no quartz in the mantle. The minerals in the mantle are very dense, and quartz is fairly light—if there ever has been any quartz in the mantle, it has long since been squeezed up to the crust. As we saw earlier, the crust makes up only a tiny portion of the earth, and it is in the crust where quartz is found. If we look at the total composition of the mantle, the most abundant mineral in the mantle by far is the mineral olivine. You are probably more familiar with olivine in its gemstone form: peridot. The amount of olivine in the mantle may exceed, by two or three times, the bulk of the entire crust!

Quartz is not even the most abundant mineral in the crust. The honours here go to the mineral feldspar, as mentioned earlier, one of the minerals that make up granite. There are hundreds of times more feldspar in the crust than quartz.

Although the exact percentages (at least to my knowledge) have never been worked out, there are other minerals that will also be more abundant than quartz; calcite for example, which is the main constituent of limestone.

It is true, however, that quartz has the largest number of *varieties*. Amethyst, citrine, smokey quartz, rock crystal, agate, jasper, adventurine, chrysoprase, etc., are all *varieties* of quartz. They are all made of silicon and oxygen, but take their variety name from their colour or texture. So, amethyst is actually quartz, but is only called amethyst because of its purple colour.

I mentioned earlier that if aluminium and oxygen were combined in the earth, the mineral was called corundum. As a mineral name, that is fairly boring: but when corundum is red in colour the *variety* is called ruby. When corundum is any other colour, especially blue, the *variety* is called sapphire. Thus, sapphire and ruby are not minerals—they are varieties of the mineral corundum.

Because quartz happens to have a large number of varieties, it doesn't make quartz special. There are *2,500* different minerals—quartz is only *one* of them.

There is no shortage of other myths about quartz, and we examine those in the context of other myths about crystals generally.

Another major myth about crystals is that they can store energy.

They can't.

A crystal by its nature is in perfect energy balance; every atom in that crystal is held very rigidly and very accurately in place by enormously well-balanced energies. If the atoms which make up the average crystal were the size of a football, then there is no way that you or I could place those football-sized atoms, even with the most accurate surveying instruments, as accurately and as precisely as they are placed inside the crystal.

If any energy comes to that crystal, it either doesn't absorb it at all, or if the energy does go into the crystal, then by its nature, it must immediately get rid of an equal amount of energy in order to keep itself in balance.

So there is *no way* you can store energy in a crystal.

One of the beliefs about why that apparently happens is what is called the piezoelectric effect. If you haven't run into that word yet, you will!

There is a lot of talk about it, particularly with quartz crystals. It comes from the idea that if you put pressure on a quartz crystal it gives off electricity. That's true, but what happens is that you are putting in X amount of mechanical energy by putting pressure on the crystal, and it gives off equally X amount of light and electric energy. But the minute you release the pressure from the crystal it reabsorbs it again. So it stays in perfect balance.

This is a property of crystals that makes them useful for watches. If you have a quartz watch you have a little quartz crystal in the watch, and a battery. The battery puts electricity into the quartz crystal; but because the quartz crystal will not absorb the energy, it has to give off an equal amount of energy to keep itself in balance; the energy it gives off is the mechanical energy of vibration. Because the atoms in crystals are so precisely placed, if you put the same electrical energy into two pieces of crystal which are exactly the same size, each crystal will give off exactly the same vibration. The rate at which a crystal vibrates per minute is known.

So, in your watch you have a little quartz crystal, a battery, and a computer that counts up the vibrations. The computer knows how many times the little piece of quartz will vibrate in a minute. When it's vibrated that many times it clicks over the minute counter; and when it's done that 60 times it clicks over the hour counter and so forth. But the energy is *not* being stored in the crystal; it's giving it off in another form.

Going back to the original idea that if we squeeze a quartz crystal we get electricity out of it—crystals are almost incompressable. The amount of pressure you can put on a quartz crystal with your hand is so tiny that it would be difficult if not impossible, even with the most accurate instruments, to measure the amount of electricity being given off. And it is *just electricity*—you can get the same stuff out of your wall socket, so there is no need to squeeze a quartz crystal to get it! In fact, crystals are so incompressable that if we were to take a quartz crystal an inch long and about a half-an-inch in diameter, and we wanted to squeeze that crystal down to about half of its original thickness, we would have to stack on top of that crystal a weight equal to approximately 5,000 railway locomotives. You can imagine how hard you have to squeeze quartz crystal to get anything out of it whatsoever!

The reason why I use quartz as an example is that you'll hear all of these various qualities that I have just given you attributed to quartz. As if quartz were the only thing that does this!

A lot of other minerals do exactly the same thing as quartz does. Most of them do to some degree, but the mineral tourmaline does all of the electronic things that quartz does *even better* than quartz. The reason we don't have tourmaline watches, or that tourmaline is not used in most other electronic applications (it is used in a few by the way), is that tourmaline is not cheap, as you've probably noticed if ever you've tried to buy a tourmaline ring. It is fifty to a hundred times more expensive than quartz. And also, at the moment, we don't know how to grow it synthetically. Almost all the quartz that is used in electronics is synthetic, all grown in the laboratory. Therefore it is relatively cheap and it does all of these things well enough. But it doesn't do them as well as tourmaline.

The other minerals that do exactly the same thing as quartz are not commonly available, nor are they as easy to grow in the laboratory.

Another myth is that quartz is used in computers, a total misunderstanding. Quartz is made from the metal silicon and the gas oxygen. The 'chips' that are used in computers and other electronics are made purely from the metal silicon. They contain no oxygen and they are *not* quartz. All of us right now are breathing the gas oxygen and it is a component of quartz, just like silicon is. But we are not breathing quartz. I think most of us are pretty aware of that. You can see by silly comparison, the myth of the idea that the silicon metal used in 'chips' is quartz. There is no connection except they just happen to have one component in common.

Another myth is that crystals have to be 'perfect' in order to be useful. Now the word 'perfect' usually is taken to mean that they have to be transparent; that they don't have any chips on them, and they've grown in a really lovely form.

Nonsense.

They can be cloudy, they can be chipped, they can be battered and beaten and they are still perfectly usable. What makes crystals do what they *can* do is their atomic structure, their pattern, their *inner nature*.

That sounds a bit like some of us, doesn't it?

Some of us are a little more battered on the outside than others, and some of us aren't quite as pretty on the outside as others, and yet inside we are all beautiful, we are all perfect, we are all whole, we are all in harmony in our deepest inner nature.

And of course that's exactly the way a crystal is. *If it wasn't perfect it wouldn't be a crystal.*

This question in fact comes up a lot in courses. My reply is: Who makes them in the first place?

God makes them doesn't he?

And does He make anything that is not perfect?

An alternative reply is: We just have to remember that God doesn't make things as perfect as man does!

By the time you have thought about *that* for a little while, you will realize what I am saying is that perfection is in the eye of the beholder. In the eye of the creator of all things, *everything is perfect.*

Maybe we need to learn how to see things that way, rather than to see the imperfections resulting from our own judgement of things.

Another term you'll run into is double termination. The word termination just means the point on a crystal, the pyramid shaped end of the crystal. In some quartz crystals (in fact you'll find it on all kinds of other crystals as well but, once again, it's usually applied to quartz), there is a point on both ends. The term for this is double terminated. There is an idea that those crystals develop both ends at the same time and are therefore something special!

Sorry, it doesn't happen that way.

Most of the double-terminated quartz crystals form when the crystal breaks off from the cavity in which it is forming and it just grows another point on the broken end. No big mystery about it at all.

Another term you'll run into are male crystals and female crystals. I'm not quite sure how you tell the difference; there is no tail to lift up.

The origin of this myth comes out of American Indian mythology and was originally connected to turquoise. In American Indian mythology, Mother Earth is seen as being green, connected to the green of growing things; and Father

Sky is seen as being blue. Turquoise comes in green and blue and therefore the green turquoise was assumed to be feminine or Mother Earth turquoise; the blue turquoise was assumed to be masculine or Father Sky turquoise.

If we ourselves embody a great deal of feminine energy we might well experience crystals giving off 'those sort of' energies; if indeed crystals gave off energy, which they don't. But they are only reflecting our own energy back to us.

We experience everything around us as reflections, whether we recognize them or not.

From a purely cynical standpoint, which also happens to be a very accurate one in this particular case, the term feminine is usually applied to quartz crystal, the milky, cloudy crystals. The crystal miners in Arkansas, Brazil, and most of the places where quartz is produced, have mountains of milky crystals around that they couldn't sell because nobody wanted them. Everyone wanted the very clear ones. Isn't it convenient that suddenly the milky crystals are 'female' and all of a sudden now they have a high market value? They couldn't *give* the things away a few years ago.

This doesn't mean that the milky ones aren't of value—they are *still crystals*, and therefore still perfect. But let's please stop our need for a lot of nonsensical terms to justify *what is*.

There is more of this by the way; the whole idea of birthstones was cooked up by the Victorian jewellery industry to sell certain stones that were in abundance at that particular time.

If any of you have looked into the lists of birthstones, you'll see that there are almost as many lists as birthstones, and they are all different! And isn't it interesting, if you trace the lists that have appeared at various times in about the last 80–90 years, the stones that appear on the list at any particular time are the ones that just happened to be quite abundant at that time!

As I mentioned earlier, a major myth is that crystals give off some kind of energy. It's impossible. There's no way a crystal can give off energy unless another energy has been put into it. They don't give off anything at all by themselves. They *can't*. Remember that the very nature of a crystal, the thing that makes it a crystal, is its perfect energy balance. If it was giving off energy, it would be putting itself out of balance. It is not the *nature* of crystals to be out of balance.

Another myth is that crystals amplify energy; that somehow they take your energy and they make it bigger. If a crystal is going to keep itself in perfect balance, there's no possible way that it can give off more energy than is put into it. It's *impossible* for a crystal to amplify energy.

There is another connection here too about amplifiers. You have an amplifier on your stereo, on your television, any sound instrument has an amplifier in it. There *are* quartz crystals in it (quartz because its cheap, otherwise it would be tourmaline), but *all* that those crystals do is control the rate of vibration in the electronics. That's *all they do*. They don't amplify, they don't magnify, they don't do *anything* but just *sit there and vibrate*.

Because they are used to control the rate of vibration in electronics, there are other myths: one of these is that they transmit energy.

Quartz crystals *are* used in radio transmitters, used once again to control the rate of vibration. If any of you have a citizens' band radio, you'll know that if you want to talk to someone on Channel 13, you need a Channel 13 crystal, and they have to have the same crystal in their radio. All that means is that the vibration given off by all Channel 13 crystals is exactly the same. This is because the crystals are exactly the same size and shape, so give off exactly the same vibrations. Channel 13 crystals anywhere in the world will have exactly the same physical dimensions and therefore they vibrate at exactly the same rate.

The crystals are not doing the transmitting. The *only* thing they are doing is *controlling the vibration*.

And if a crystal comes along that is cheaper than quartz, or if it ever becomes cheap to grow tourmaline in the laboratory, we'll use these instead. If we can find some way to make old banana skins vibrate at such a precise rate, we'll use them instead of crystals.

Why do myths happen? How do they get started?

We know that things can have the appearance of doing one thing, when in fact something entirely different is happening. We are deceived by appearances.

There are things that happen with crystals that *appear* to amplify, that *appear* to transmit, that *appear* to heal, that appear to do quite a few things. But what's really happening is that our own *human ability* to heal, our own *human ability* to amplify, to focus our own energies, is being *reflected back to us* more clearly through the use of crystals.

We can take any number of personal development courses and the one thing which we will learn in every single one of those courses is that **clear intentions get clear results**.

What greater reflection back to us of the most subtle and profound levels of our own inner clarity could there be than the very clearest expression of energy that exists in the universe: the crystal. When we hold crystals, when we use crystals, when we have them near us, we have reflections back to us at an intuitive level of our own inner clarity. When we form an intention coming from that most powerful level of clarity in ourselves, then we get clear results.

And it *looks* as if somehow the crystal has done it.

Crystals don't do anything except reflect. Just like everything else outside of yourself.

People are powerful, *people* are healing, *people* are all of the things that we think crystals are. All the crystals do is reflect back to us. And, as such, they are immensely powerful *tools* for healing at a most subtle and deep level. But they are not doing the actual healing—this comes solely from inside ourselves.

Because we are out of touch with our Inner Being, the source of our own healing, our own power, when we see those things reflected back to us in crystals we don't recognize them as reflections because we don't recognize them in ourselves.

We believe that the reflection is the reality.

Throughout this book, you can use those reflections to become more and more in touch with the reality of who You really are.

Basic Crystal Use

I am frequently asked about various aspects of the use of crystals, especially that of 'cleansing' and 'programming'. You will find an enormous amount of information available on these two subjects in various books, and there are nearly as many techniques as there are books. In truth, it doesn't matter what activity you undertake in any of these processes, as it is not the activity itself that is creating the response. As in all things in the world, it is solely a result of your intention.

As I have been talking about the mirroring effect of crystals throughout this text, I think it will be helpful to look at the various stages of crystal use in those terms.

The first term is called **cleansing**. If crystals are mirrors of the Self, then cleansing is nothing more than cleaning the mirror! Physical mirrors get fingerprints on them, they get cloudy, they get dusty—in other words they need to be cleaned in order to see a clear reflection. Crystals as mirrors are exactly the same.

What crystals are mirroring is energy, and therefore the reflections they give are energetic in nature. Likewise, that which keeps a crystal from giving a clear reflection is also energetic, and therefore the 'cleaning' of a crystal also takes place at an energetic level.

As has been discussed, a crystal does not store energy, and yet, through its contact with the human kingdom, there is some sort of energetic shift that takes place within it, a change of consciousness. This can be a result of being dug from the earth originally, from being handled by the miner, the various crystal dealers who have sold and resold it, or other people who have handled it or whose thoughts and intentions have been impressed upon it.

The act of cleaning, then, is nothing more than returning the consciousness of the crystal, returning its reflectivity, to whatever state you wish it to be in. Often, this is returning a crystal to its natural consciousness, as it resided in the earth. At other times a crystal will be 'programmed' and it will be desired to leave that programme in the crystal. Programming will be discussed in the next stage.

Above all, it must be remembered that the physical activity of cleaning, whatever it may be, is not actually what has happened. The crystal is responding to the intention of the cleaner, and whatever physical activity is being used is merely a reinforcement of the intention of the person doing the cleaning, and it is that intention that the crystal is responding to.

So, put it in the moonlight, soak it in salt water, wipe it with eucalyptus oil, or whatever. Whatever activity you wish to perform, reinforce *your* intention about the state of being of the crystal, about the clarity of the reflections it gives back to you.

My own method for cleaning is to use a simple visualization, as all that is really necessary to clean a crystal is a focused intention. For me, a symbol of purity is clear mountain spring water, so I just visualize a flow of that water through the crystal, washing away anything that I don't want in the crystal. With an unprogrammed crystal, I visualize it washing away anything that was not part of the original nature of the crystal: but with a programmed crystal, I intend for it to retain its original nature plus whatever programme I have in it.

Programming is the act of selecting whatever reflection you wish to have come back to you from the crystal. So, when we programme a crystal for healing, we are really programming that crystal to reflect back to us our own human ability and capacity to balance and harmonize. Or, if we are using a crystal in a clinical situation, we are using it to reflect to the patient their own natural abilities for self-healing. Once again, it is our intention that is creating the action here, and a crystal is merely acting as a reflector.

If you programme a crystal for meditation, then you are selecting a reflection back to you of some higher aspect of yourself. We exist on many different levels, and it takes a bit of effort to bring some of those levels into our conscious mind. This is the function of meditation.

Another stage could be called **protection**. Once again, the protection stage is nothing more than being selective about the reflections, and in this case reflections which we don't wish it to give. My particular protective programme is to install the thought in the crystal that I don't wish it to reflect anything that is not in harmony with the Christ energy. There are a lot of energies around in the world, energies at many different levels of life and different levels of being. The Christ energy is an energy that applies solely to the human race, but all other energies in the world are in harmony with it. If we think about it for a minute, the *only* unharmonious energies in the world are those created by the human race!

There is no reason whatever why all of these steps cannot be performed with a single thought, but in the beginning it helps to break things down into stages. Many of you will be using crystals already, and are undoubtedly familiar with these steps, and have perhaps developed your own variations on them. As long as you are clear in your intention, the actual form that these various steps take is irrelevant.

In choosing the crystal for whatever purpose required, I have seen all sorts of methods proposed and demonstrated for doing this—bent coat hangers, muscle testing, etc. There is certainly nothing wrong with any of these, but as we are really looking into our own hearts, I always suggest that in using crystals, we do precisely that! Every one of us deep inside ourselves has some sort of body feeling or sensation, usually associated with the heart, or sometimes the solar plexus, that says: 'This feels right'. In choosing crystals, I always suggest that you simply go for the 'feels right' feeling.

In choosing a crystal, you are really looking for one that resonates in some way with your Inner Being. If you were choosing a crystal to reflect the healing aspect of yourself, then one particular crystal above others may resonate to that. Likewise with meditation, one particular crystal will resonate.

Perhaps you have had the experience of going to a table filled with crystals, and there is one crystal on the table that 'speaks' to you. This is a crystal that is in some way like you—a perfect outworking of the universal law that says 'like attracts like'.

I always suggest that people should choose and programme crystals for themselves. There are certianly a lot of people around who will offer to do both for you, but your deepest Inner Being always knows best about what is right for you. What we are all ultimately working toward in this life is taking full responsibility for ourselves and for our own lives, and this is another small way in which you can begin to do that. So what if you make a mistake? There is no way you can harm yourself with crystals anyway.

Another frequently asked question is 'should crystals that we are using be kept away from others, kept separately?' Once again, the answer is do whatever feels right. Many people *do* feel that certain crystals that are especially for their personal use, such as crystals used in meditation or self-healing, are more appropriately kept by themselves, but again it is not a definite rule. This doesn't imply, by the way, that there is any-thing secretive or mysterious about this process—every human being has a need for privacy, and this will just be an extension of that need.

4   The Crystal Heart

So, at last we begin some exercises.

To remind you again, I recommend that you keep a notebook to write down all of the details that come to you during the various exercises, and to gauge your own progress, and also, that you put the instructions of these exercises on tape, so that you can follow them through with the minimum of interruption.

The first part of this chapter is given to supplementary techniques, which you may find useful at any time during the remaining exercises of this book.

Supplementary Techniques

There are several techniques here that do not directly use crystals. However, as many of the crystal techniques involve working through energy blockages, all of the supplementary techniques can be used to good advantage at any time during the clearing process. **All blockages are a restriction of your own life force. Rage is nothing more than blocked life energy.**

It is inevitable, therefore, that as deeper and deeper releasings take place you will experience a great deal of rage and anger, often seeming at times unconnected to any surrounding events. Or you will create events in your life that justify the feelings. Recognize that all you are experiencing is your own primal instinct for survival, and that any blockage to the full flow of your own life force will come out as rage or anger. Therefore, the first three techniques involve opening the chakras to a rich and full expression of rage. These releases are quite healthy and, if you have had a clean release, you will feel good afterwards. This is the clearest indication that you have actually released blocked energy. If not, you have probably not opened the chakras fully and should keep repeating the technique you are using until you feel good afterwards. The other indications of energy release mentioned elsewhere in the text also apply.

It is important to realize that persons or events which bring up the feeling of rage in you are merely acting as symbols or triggers for the primal childhood events which created the blockages in the first place. Blaming the person or event in the current time for your feelings is inappropriate, as this person or event has merely served to reflect back to you your own blockage. It is, however, perfectly okay to use this person or event as a symbol, and in doing these progresses to imagine that you are actually striking or venting your anger at that person.

Once you have done a release it is amazing how differently you will view the events which brought up the feeling of rage in the first place. You will find in many instances that the feeling in retrospect was quite irrational. And yet in the moment before the release the feeling may have felt so intense as to feel life-threatening. When you have cleanly released the feelings through the techniques, you will also find that you will begin to experience an increasing degree of forgiveness for the person who has 'caused' the feeling, with the ultimate goal in mind to stop blaming other people for your feelings, and just own them as your own.

Supplementary Technique 1

Life flat on the bed, or, if one is not available, a thick pile of mats. You will want a good deal of padding here, as you are going to be kicking with your full strength.

If you have an opportunity to notice an infant in a crib, when his needs are going unmet, he will be kicking furiously away! It is also quite natural for small children to kick out in anger, either at adults or their contemporaries! In raising children, the kicking impulse is inhibited very early on, so much so that in America it even has an equivalent form of speech:

'How are you feeling John?'
'Oh, I can't kick.' (' I can't complain.')

The technique is done lying on the bed, then, and by raising one leg and the opposite arm as high as possible, and kicking down with the heel and striking downward with a clenched fist as hard as possible, putting the full force of your anger or rage into the kick. It also helps if you can verbalize your feelings at this time, either by visualizing and directing a 'comment' to the person who has 'caused' your feelings, or by growling or making some other noise deep in the throat. It is important to make a noise here as it opens the upper chakras, and permits a clean flow of energy throughout the body.

Then, raise the other leg and opposite arm, and once again strike and kick downward with all of your might. Continue doing this, alternating from leg to leg and arm to arm until you have exhausted yourself and/or the feeling has disappeared.

You may find that you will alternate between periods of deep crying, and deep rage. There will often be a great deal of grief locked up within the same energy.

When the feeling has passed, roll on to your left side and cover yourself to keep warm, and allow your body to reintegrate. You will either begin feeling good and feel like getting out of bed, or you may find that additional feelings will arise, and it may be necessary to repeat the exercise several times.

This is a very powerful exercise, and you may even find that it will be difficult for you to do it in the beginning, as you may find it almost impossible to kick! This impulse is so deeply inhibited that you may actually have to fake it in order to get started.

Supplementary Technique   2

Sometimes it is not appropriate or possible to kick heavily as in the previous exercise, so I suggest that you do 'kickettes'. These are little short kicks raising the heels only a few inches above the bed, and done very rapidly alternating from leg to leg. These are a great deal less noisy, and will still be very useful for releasing, although the release is not quite as deep as the Technique Number 1.

Supplementary Technique 3

This is a technique for striking with the arms, but doing so in a way that is unlikely to cause you physical harm. While the kicking techniques are important for your deep and primal rage, there is also a natural urge to strike out with the arms and hands. The instructions for this technique are a bit more complicated, and it is important to do this correctly, otherwise this technique can degenerate into wallowing behaviour very quickly, as in a child striking out in a tantrum.

As shown in Figure 4, kneel alongside a bed or a chair with a solid cushion. If you are using a chair, make sure that it has at least 6 inches of cushion and spring, as you will be striking very hard.

Figure 4a Pelvis forward/shoulders back/chest expanded/ head back/throat stretched/body weight supported on thighs

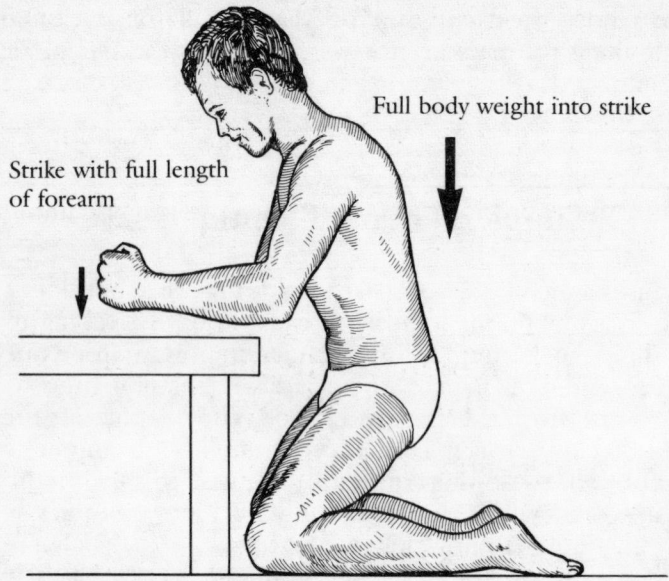

Full body weight into strike

Strike with full length
of forearm

Figure 4b

The body is tilted backward in an arch, as if the body
is in the curvature of a bow being drawn. The pelvis is
tilted upward, the shoulders are back and the chest is
expanded, and the head is also tilted back, with the
throat stretched and the mouth open wide. This opens
all of the chakras, and permits a clear flow of energy
through the body. The weight of the body is supported
on the thighs. The fists are clenched, and are held
approximately over the shoulders.

The striking motion is done by coming downward
with the full body weight, and striking the bed or chair
along the full length of the forearm, rather than using
the fists. **If you strike with your fists only, you may
injure your wrists**. Practise this a few times in slow
motion before trying it with full force.

It is important to stretch the body fully in the arch
before each strike, otherwise this exercise will degenerate into wallowing. You will be able to put enormous
force into the blow, so be certain that the chair or bed is
quite solid and well padded.

As you do the exercise, it is perfectly appropriate to visualize striking the person against whom you are feeling deep rage, always recognizing that that person is merely serving to bring up feelings which already exist within you.

These exercises are in no way intended to stimulate violence against actual persons.

As with the previous exercises, repeat this exercise until the feeling of rage has passed, and/or you have had a deep crying release.

Supplementary Technique   4
The Towel Twist

This exercise is done by folding or rolling a towel until your hands fit comfortably around it. The hands should be placed 6 to 8 inches apart, with both hands on top of the twist, and the thumbs towards the body, as in Figure

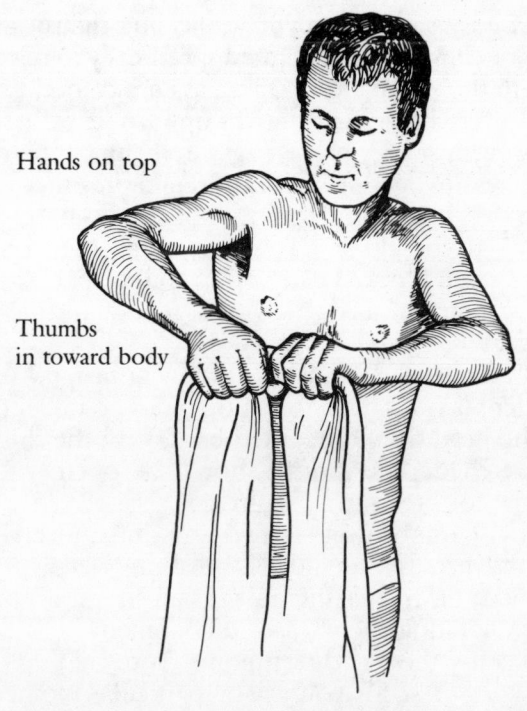

Hands on top

Thumbs
in toward body

Figure 5

5. The technique is done by simply twisting the towel,
as if you are wringing water out of it. Or, as if you are
wringing someone's neck! And while you are doing so,
making a growling noise deep in the throat will help to
break loose the energy block.

This exercise can be done kneeling or standing, and if you
practise it a bit you will soon discover that you can put your
full body weight into the twisting, especially using the muscles
of the shoulders and upper torso.

This is a wonderful exercise as it can be done anywhere;
you can even slip into the bathroom at someone else's house
during a party if necessary. Obviously, the amount of growling you will wish to do is optional!

Supplementary Technique   5

This exercise is useful when you are feeling tightness in
the throat or chest, and is designed specifically to release
blockages in those two areas. Often, as energy is released
from the lower chakras and moves upward, it will tend
to come up against energy blockages in the upper part of
the body, creating feelings of tension and pressure. It is
almost the 'feel like crying' feeling. In fact, this is exactly
what needs to be done. However, since the crying
response is often blocked early on as well (especially in
men), we sometimes need to give our natural instincts a
bit of help.

For this exercise, lie flat, with a pillow just supporting
the shoulder blades. The pillow should not go under the
head, as the head should be tilted back, with the throat
slightly stretched. The mouth should be open, wider
than normal for breathing (Figure 6).

The exercise can be done in two ways: first, by taking
deep breaths through the mouth, breathing deeply into
the abdomen; or, by making an aaaaaah sound deep in
the throat, vibrating the chest and abdomen.

By alternating these two techniques, you will find the
one that works best for you at any particular moment.
This technique will often produce a deep crying release,
occasionally triggering a deep coughing as if there is

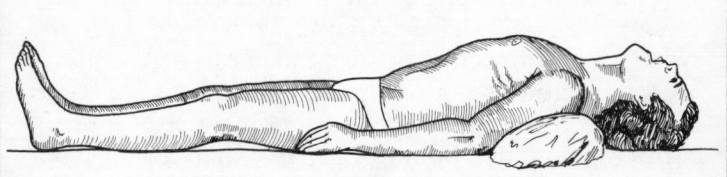

Elements of drawing:
Pillow under shoulders
Head back/throat stretched/mouth wide

Figure 6

something in your lungs that you are desperately trying
to get out. This is often exactly the case, because when
the umbilical cord is cut too quickly the infant will often
be left struggling to breathe, and, as panic sets in, a per-
manent restriction of the breathing will result. What
you are actually doing when this deep coughing is triggered is trying to clear your lungs of amniotic fluid (at
least psychologically). This is a very healthy response
and it can be triggered by any number of exercises in this
book. You will find that as it occurs, your own capacity
for breathing will become deeper and deeper, and a
great feeling of aliveness will begin to infuse your body.
This will often be accompanied by tingling sensations,
especially in the limbs. It is not unlike the feeling of
blood returning to your foot when you have had your
leg curled up underneath you, restricting your circulation. But in this case your circulation is being freed by
the removal of an energy block, and it is the feeling of
life returning more fully to your body.

Supplementary Technique   6
Mantras

A technique that I have found useful for discovering
energy blockages in the chakras is through the use of my
Mantra. Many of you will already be doing meditations

using a Mantra, which is a word or group of words that produce a particular resonance somewhere within you. If you are already using a Mantra, then use it in this process; if you do not have a Mantra, then you can use the syllable OM, or even your own name can be used. The Mantra is either sung or chanted, in order to give it a resonant quality. To practise sounding the Mantra in each of the chakra points, I suggest that you do your Mantra aloud, and first of all be conscious of the vibration at the throat and chest. Then, as you sound the Mantra again and again, try sensing its vibration in each of the chakra points, starting from the base chakra and working upwards.

After you have done it verbally for a while, then try closing your eyes in a meditative state, and just sound your Mantra internally, but without making any audible sounds. In other words, feel it as an internal vibration, rather than a physical one. Again, feel it first in the throat and chest, where you would feel the physical vibrations first; then go once again from chakra to chakra, 'sounding' your Mantra in each chakra.

Any energy blockages in any of the chakras will feel as if there is an inhibiting effect on the full vibration of the Mantra in whichever chakra is affected. Often just sounding the Mantra in the blocked chakra will cause energy release but, if not, use your crystal over the chakra point and move the blocked energy up into the heart centre as in the Energy Moving exercise.

Often an energy blockage in the chakra can be felt as heat radiating from the body. To sense this, move your hand up and down the front on your body if you are doing it on yourself, or up and down the back if doing it on someone else. Do this with your hand 2 to 4 inches from the body. You will notice temperature changes radiate from the body, and the places where you feel the greatest amount of heat are the places where energy blockages occur. If an energy blockage has been identified by this method, placing a crystal in the warmest area and stroking upward toward the throat will begin to move the energy block upward. This type of auric massage is likely to create emotional release.

You can be certain that you have had a genuine energy release through emotional catharsis if there is a feeling of heat being released from the body. An intense release will produce intense sweating and a feeling as if the body temperature has risen considerably. Often, in the moments before a release takes place, the body will feel highly chilled as the body withdraws its energy to protect itself as the fear begins to rise. A feeling of chill, with shivering or shaking, should be taken as a sign that energy is trying to release itself, and you should allow whatever feelings are present in the body at that time to develop further. The sensations that accompany uncomfortable emotions being released are often in themselves uncomfortable; however, the object is not at the moment to make it feel better. In fact, until a clean emotional release takes place, uncomfortable feelings should be made to feel *worse*!

It is only by getting *into* these feelings, that they can finally be released. To attempt to soothe or calm them before they are released only keeps them stuck.

After an emotional release has taken place, there may well be a desire to soothe, and, in doing this, the hand should be moved along the spine from the throat downward, again 'stroking' the aura from 2 to 4 inches from the body. After a powerful emotional release, lie on your left side in the foetal position and allow the new body state to integrate. The integration feeling will be a feeling of energy returning to the body with a sense of calmness and clarity, and a feeling of desire to get on with whatever comes next. It may be necessary to go through several stages of release and integration in order for this feeling to occur. If you are lying in the foetal position and still experiencing uncomfortable feelings there is probably yet another stage of release to go through.

It is also important to remember that once the releasing process begins, emotional feelings may begin rising to the surface for some period of weeks or months afterwards. And, after an intense emotional release, you may feel tired or sleepy as the muscle tension which held those energies in place relaxes.

A lower level of emotional release, a release which is almost a 'wallowing' in the feeling state, will usually fail to produce a feeling of heat radiating from the body. If you are experiencing this sort of release, you need to go much deeper into your feelings. It is also desirable, but not absolutely necessary, to have another person with you while you go through these processes. Your own sense of trust and safety in having another person present while you are in what is often such a vulnerable state, will be your guide as to its appropriateness. Remember though that if you are working with someone with whom you are in a close relationship, as your issues come up, *their* issues will be triggered! Therefore the person who is working with you should be aware of their own feelings that are arising, and it may be a necessary agreement of your relationship that you both have personal space and time to work with these issues without the necessity to do them with one another. The largest psychological hazard here is to get into blaming each other for the feelings that are arising, and you should both be aware of that tendency if you do work together. Remember your feelings are *yours*, and your partner's feelings are *theirs*.

The first crystal exercises begin working directly with the heart centre. The first three are about gradually going deeper and deeper into your heart centre, to begin firstly to connect with it, and secondly to discover what resides there.

The first exercise is about cleansing the heart centre, and is designed to set in motion, subconsciously, powerful energetic forces in your own Being that will facilitate the remaining exercises in this book.

The human mind works very much in symbols, and by creating appropriate symbols our subconscious mind will grasp them very quickly, and begin making the preceptual shifts that are necessary for our further opening. The first exercise is designed to do this:

Heart Cleansing

Purpose:
This is an exercise for symbolically cleansing the heart centre. In it you are using the crystal as a symbol of the perfect Inner Being that dwells in the depth of your heart. We will be using a visualization technique to clear away anything that is clouding the perfect Inner Being— all thoughts, feelings, and beliefs that are not in perfect harmony with who you are. This will all be seen in symbols; you may see inharmonious beliefs as tiny bits of rubbish, as black gunk, or as some sort of debris scat-

tered about; just let your own mind create whatever symbol works the best for you.

Crystal:
The crystal for this exercise will be placed directly over the heart centre and in the exercise you will be projecting yourself into the crystal. In choosing a crystal for this exercise find one with which you feel a deep heart connection.

Programme:
This crystal is programmed to reflect back to you the deepest levels of your own perfection, and, by contrast, to be able to see all of those things in your heart, in whatever symbols are appropriate, that keep it from being clear and clean and a perfect source of love to all of your being.

With the crystal in place over your heart, take in a few deep breaths and let them out slowly. As you do, become aware of your own heartbeat. Focus initially on the heartbeat, rather than the crystal. As you become more and more focused on your heartbeat, feel that heartbeat as the centre of your being, as if everything that you are is focused in that beat. And as you become more and more focused on the heart, then extend your awareness to include the crystal resting on it.

As you become more and more focused on the crystal, visualize the crystal becoming larger and larger, and your body becoming smaller and smaller. Eventually the crystal will become larger than your body, and you can then allow yourself to slip inside the crystal. It is as if we are stepping inside your own heart, the symbol of which is the crystal.

When you are inside the crystal, take a moment to sense the feeling of utter balance and perfection inside, and take a moment to just look around. Experience being in your crystal as if being inside a room—the facets of the crystal are the walls of the room.

And when you feel comfortable inside, notice that in one of the walls of the room (one of the faces of the crystal) there is a window. You can see this as any sort of window you like—a porthole, a large window, a small window—but in any instance one that can be opened.

So, walk to the window and open it. And as you look out of the window, you will see that what is outside is . . . the Cosmos. A whole universe of stars outside the window.

The universe is the source of everything in our Being—the unbalanced thoughts and beliefs, as well as the balanced ones. Our unbalanced thoughts and feelings are ones which have taught us: they are the things which have propelled us into learning. But as we begin to reach out to reharmonize ourselves with the universe, we no longer need these things, so it's okay to return them to the universe.

So, now have a look around inside your heart crystal, looking for anything that looks out of balance, anything that is not in harmony. As I mentioned, you may see it as rubbish or litter, or of some sort of muck. You will find at hand whatever tools you need to clean with, so set to it! And as you clean up whatever rubbish you find inside, just shovel it out of the window, return it to the Cosmos.

And as you go on cleaning, you will see the whole place becoming tidier; it may have begun to take on a bright and shiny brand-new sort of look. You may even want to take a cloth and polish it!

When you have finished cleaning, then close up your window and return your cleaning tools to the proper place.

When you have completed all of this, begin taking deeper and deeper breaths focusing on your heartbeat. As you do so, visualize the crystal becoming smaller and smaller and your body becoming larger and larger, until you have both returned to your proper size.

Use this meditation any time that feelings of negativity arise. And on completing this meditation, take out your notebook, and record in as much detail as possible all that you can remember.

The cave is an important symbol for the heart centre, for as you go deeper and deeper into the body of the earth in a real cave, you go deeper and deeper into the body of your own

Being in a symbolic cave. This exercise is designed around the
self-reflective power of crystals, and is a good beginning at
truly looking at yourself, and what is really there.

The Crystal Cave

Purpose:
This is an exercise for deep self-exploration. It is for
getting deep into the heart centre and for taking a clear
look at yourself—including your own Shadow.

Crystal:
Place the crystal on the heart centre. Use a crystal that
almost feels as if it were a physical mirror that you could
actually look into and see a physical reflection of yourself.

Programme:
The programme for this crystal is to give a clear reflection
of what is deep in your own heart—the rough with the
smooth.

To begin this exercise, find yourself in a place out of
doors, a place that might, for you, embody the words
'The Earth'. A place where you might find the entrance
to a cave.

Create the day to be a day that you would be happy to
return to—sun shining, birds singing and so forth.

This cave you are going to explore is a warm and dry
cave, and well lighted. And what you will see as you go
deeper into the cave is that the walls of the cave are lined
with crystals, crystals of all sorts of sizes, shapes and
colours.

As you walk into the entrance of the cave you will
notice the floor slopes downward, so as you walk further
into the cave you will be walking deeper and deeper into
the earth. As you do, feel the living rock surrounding
you.

The light at the entrance will gradually disappear
behind you, as you begin to notice the crystals lining the
walls of the cave—reflecting, sparkling, pure and pefect.

Allow yourself plenty of time to get very deeply into

the cave, and when you are as deep as you wish to go, feel yourself in a large room, elongated like a central corridor of the cave. And from this central room there will be little crystal-lined rooms, little grottoes, opening to the left and to the right.

Before you begin to explore these rooms, it is important to have a clear intention to remember what you see, as there are several rooms to explore.

The first one that you will explore is the chamber to the right of the central corridor. As you look into that chamber you will see it lined with crystals, and as you go into that room to begin to explore you will see certain specific reflections coming back to you from those crystals. You may see them as visual reflections, or you may feel them as psychic or intuitive reflections. What these crystals will be reflecting back to you are the best parts of yourself, your most positive characteristics, your most positive traits. Give yourself a few minutes to explore this chamber.

When you have seen all you wish to see, return to the central corridor of the cave, bringing with you memories of as many reflections as you could find in the room of positive reflections.

Go now to the little room opening to the left of the central corridor where once again you will see a room lined with crystals. These crystals will also reflect something of yourself back to you, but in this room they will reflect the parts of yourself you really don't like to look at, your shadow self. As you go in and explore those reflections, also be aware that many of those reflections of the disharmonious parts of you have also been very important learning experiences for you. And, until you identify and learn to love, and learn to work with those parts of yourself, you can never be a complete being. The shadow self serves as a vital part of who you are, and it is not a self to be done away with—it is a self to be embraced, and integrated. Coming to accept ourselves as we really are is the *only* path to enlightenment and self-healing. So, when you have completed your exploration of the room of difficult reflections, return to the central portion of the cave.

Once back in the central corridor, you will notice the cave goes even deeper into the earth and, as you follow the cave further downward, you will notice the crystals get more and more beautiful. And the reflections that come back to you are even more beautiful and profound, because these crystals, in the deepest part of your being, will reflect back to you the True You, the real Self. Follow the cave downward as deeply as you can, until you come to the place where the largest and most beautiful crystals of all are, and you will see in those crystals reflected back to you, the great Cosmic Being that you really are.

And when you have completed the exploration of that deepest portion of the cave, begin your way back upward, climbing until you reach the surface, until you return to the bright beautiful day outdoors, on this beautiful place called The Earth.

In the exercise that follows, you will use the symbol of a cave once again, but this time with the Sacred Spring. As in the previous exercise, you will use the cave symbol to go deeply into the core of your own Being, but this time in the core of your being you will experience the Well Spring of your own life. The depth of inner connection you can make in this exercise is profound, and it is one that you may wish to repeat a number of times as you progress along your inward journey. What you will discover as you do so is that the inner experience, although similar or identical in form each time, will have more subtle nuances, connecting with deeper subtleties of your own Being.

The Sacred Spring

Purpose:
To be in touch with the deepest level of your own heart, the energy pattern that is at the core of your Being.

Crystal:
Choose a crystal for this exercise to which you feel a response deep in your heart centre. I suggest you look for a physical sensation in the heart for this one. In this exercise, the crystal is placed over the heart.

Programme:
To be drawn into the very deepest level of your own
Being, and to see reflected back to you, the energy pat-
tern that is your Beingness.

In ancient times, the water source for a city was often
within the city walls, and reached through a very deep
well. These wells were often more than just vertical
shafts—they were proper tunnels, with stairs leading
down into them. Our sacred spring will be in such a
location.

Go in your mind then to some ancient place—a place
where you feel a sacred connection. This can be a real
place or an imagined one. Whatever place you go to,
find a doorway, a doorway that opens into a sloping
tunnel, that leads to a sacred spring. Create the kind of
doorway you might expect to find in such a place: an
elaborate doorway, the entrance to a temple, or whatever image you would see for such a sacred place.

As you walk up to the door, you may sense that you
would like to do some sort of ritual, or some sort of personal cleansing as you are about to enter a holy place.
When you have done so, enter the doorway and begin
walking downward. There is a passageway, a sloping
tunnel that leads deep into the earth. It is a wide
passageway, with stairs and a slope that is comfortable to
walk down. It is warm and dry in this passageway, and it
is spacious enough that there is no sense of confinement.

As the light of day fades behind you, the lighting in
the passageway will be provided by candles, giving it a
warm and soft glow. You will hear the echo of your
footsteps, as you go deeper and deeper into the earth.

Give yourself plenty of time on this, and really try to
sense the depth—deeper, and deeper, and deeper, and
deeper.

Eventually, when you feel you have reached the very
depths, you will begin to hear a gentle sound of water
trickling. You know that you are approaching the sacred
spring, and the pool that lies at its feet. As you reach the
deepest part of the tunnel, you will find that it opens
into a large room, with a beautiful pool of candlelit
water, surrounded by a sandy beach, and by a number of

seats which surround the pool. You are there by your-self, but you know that this is the same life source for many.

Seat yourself next to the pool, and just feel the energy that comes upward with the spring—the waters of life. As you watch the pool, you will eventually notice that there is a faint glow in the water which begins to get brighter as you watch it. You know that there is no fear about what you are going to see, but you certainly may have other feelings that are appropriate to express.

The glow becomes even brighter and you suddenly sense that something is rising out of the water from the very depths. And as you watch, a glowing figure rises from the water. It is not in human form, being made up mostly of points of light, but you will be aware that radiating from this figure of light is an intense feeling of joy and love. You will realize, that in the depths of your Being, this is who you really are.

There may be some communication from this Being of light, or there may not, but in either case there will be a moment when you sense you have been in the presence of this Being for a sufficient amount of time. At that time, the Being will sink into the depths once again, leaving you alone in the candlelit chamber.

When you sense completion, allow yourself time to digest your experience, and when you are ready, return to the surface. Allow yourself plenty of time to return to the surface, and if you have experienced any deep emotional feelings throughout this experience, lie down on the bed or the floor, or wherever you are meditating, lie on your left side and allow the experience to integrate.

And be certain to write in your notebook as soon as possible after completing this experience, again writing down every detail you can remember, whether those details seem important at the moment or not.

Having made the deeper energetic connections, you will now come outward, to begin making connection with the physical body. In the following chapters there will be a cer-tain amount of work with the body, unlocking blocked energies, and allowing the life force to flow more freely through it. But for the moment, just concentrate on making

contact with your own body, and becoming more familiar
with various aspects of it.

Loving the Body

Purpose:
To be in touch with the various parts and aspects of our
physical body, and to make the energetic connection
with those parts necessary for experiencing full aliveness.

Crystal:
A crystal that gives you a sensation of 'groundedness'.
The crystal in this experience is placed on each body
part in turn, as that body part is being experienced.

Programme:
To make subtle energetic connections throughout the
body, and to reintegrate any separations that have taken
place energetically through the body.

For this exercise, lie on the floor or on the bed, with or
without clothes as you wish. To do the exercise, the
crystal is placed on each portion of the body in turn, and
time is taken to experience through the crystal the
reflection of the function of that particular part of the
body in your life.

For example, place the crystal on your right foot
(you'll have to do this one with the knees bent), and
then let the 'consciousness' of your foot be reflected
back to you from the crystal. In other words, experience
the 'footness' of whichever foot the crystal is on. Then,
take a moment to remember pleasurable times in your
life where your foot has played a major part—a walk
through a favourite place, climbing a hill, stepping out
of a train, or a bus, or a plane, to meet a loved one, etc.
Then, take a moment to thank your foot for the good
service it is giving you, all of the places it has taken you,
and all of the good things in your life that have related
to being able to stand, walk, and so forth.

Then move the crystal to the ankle, experience your
own 'ankleness' and likewise go through various times

in your life when your ankle has given you support, and pleasure. And so forth up the body.

Where the arms and legs are concerned, do them separately, and see if there is any difference in the experience of the left- and right-hand side of the body. The right side of the body tends to be associated with masculinity, and tensions and pressures on the right side tend to deal with father issues; and the reverse on the left side. The knees are particularly important, as this is one of the main areas of energetic blockage to do with parent issues.

You may wish to draw a diagram of your own body in your notebook, making note of your body responses as you do the exercise.

Having contacted the body in this exercise, it's now time to go to a higher level of energy, the energies connected with the upper energy centres. In doing the next exercise, you will be meeting a wise Being, and it is important to remember that the person you are meeting is yourself. This is not some disincarnate entity, not a spirit guide, not a person *outside yourself*. It is, in a sense, a projection of the Being at the deepest level of your own heart, but that Being projected into human form. It is the person that you have the potential to become, a person in full manifestation of their own Humanity.

The Pyramid of the Self

Purpose:
To be in contact with your Higher Self.

Crystal:
This is a crystal to go on the brow chakra, so choose a crystal that will reflect back to you your own highest level of clarity.

Programme:
The programme is to reflect back to you the highest levels of your own consciousness, and to enable you to constructively communicate with those levels.

To begin the exercise, you will find yourself out of doors, in some location where you will find a pyramid. This could be in the sacred precinct of an ancient city, it could be an Atlantean temple, or this pyramid may just exist in the middle of grassy fields—whatever image gives you a feeling of comfort and safety. And a feeling of the sacred, as you will be meeting on the top of this pyramid a very ancient and wise being, one who has the answers to the mysteries of your own life.

Approach the pyramid in whatever manner seems appropriate to you. You may find yourself dressed in robes, or you may find yourself in ordinary attire. Once again, choose whatever lends itself to your sense of impending connection with something important in your own life.

As you approach the pyramid you will see that it has a lengthy staircase leading to the top. At various levels of the pyramid there will be places where you can stop and rest, and catch your breath if necessary.

Set the scene for the day in some detail—the amount of sunshine, the location of the sun in the sky, the scent of the air, the surrounding sounds.

Allow yourself plenty of time for the climb—this is a meeting you have been waiting for for a very long time, so a few minutes more to be totally focused on the event will not go amiss.

As you begin to climb, allow yourself the physical sensation of feeling your legs move as you climb from one step to the next. Hear the sound of your shoes or sandals or feel your bare feet on the steps, and be aware that as you climb, your vista of the location surrounding the pyramid will become larger.

You will find that there are seven levels to the pyramid, and, as you reach each level, you will probably want to stop and catch your breath. At each level, you may see that there are boxes full of flowers, and each level will have flowers of a different colour. If colour aids you in visualization, you will find that the flowers in the first level are red, proceeding upwards in the rainbow colours through each level.

As you reach the top level, you will see that the top of the pyramid is a broad platform upon which is resting a gateway, a gateway made entirely of crystal. You will know that this gateway is the door to another dimension, another dimension of yourself. And, waiting on the other side of the doorway, will be a wise and ancient person, a person who is your Higher Self.

So, approach the gateway, and when you are ready, step through. It is as if you are stepping inside a crystal—a feeling of total balance, total harmony, and total crystal clarity.

On the other side of the doorway, you will find that the platform of the pyramid, being in a different dimension, appears to extend endlessly in all directions. And yet at the same time the sky is above you, the air is crisp and clear and the sun is shining brightly. And, in the distance, stands a figure.

This figure will walk towards you. Greet this person in whatever way feels appropriate. You will find that you can converse quite clearly with this person, and you will find answers here that you have been seeking about your own life.

When you have finished your conversation, walk back outwards through the crystal doorway, and you will find yourself back in the same dimension as the pyramid, back at the material level of reality, although still on a high plane. Gently begin climbing downward, until you reach the bottom of the pyramid, and plant your feet firmly on the earth once again.

As soon as your eyes are open, record at once any details of the conversation you had with your wise Being.

Having gone to a very high level of your own Beingness in this exercise, the following exercise is designed to demonstrate to you the difference between the highest and most subtle levels of your Being, and the part of your Being that is directly connected to the matter of this planet. By contrast, it is intended to show you how far you have travelled to be able to wear a physical body, and, as a result of that great distance travelled, why a certain amount of inner connection was lost at some point in your life (see also the last chapter).

Descent into Matter

Purpose:
To experience directly the extreme density of the first
body, and to put you into closer connection with the
material world around you.

Crystal:
A crystal that feels as if it embodies the words 'The
Earth'.

Programme:
To reflect back to you the energy connections of your
lower two chakras and their connection to the energies
of the earth.

Sit in a chair with your feet firmly on the ground, or in
the lotus position. The crystal should be placed as near
as possible to the base chakra. Begin breathing very
deeply, pulling the breath as low into the abdomen as
possible. As you breathe more and more into the abdomen, begin to feel as if the intake of breath is swelling
the genital area. As you become more and more in
touch with the sensations in the lower portion of the
body, allow your consciousness to sink downward
through your body, until your full awareness is in the
lower two energy centres. As you do this, you may
become aware of an intense heaviness of the rest of the
body, and while you are in this state, try to lift your arm.
You may well find that it is difficult or almost impossible
to move it.

   While you are in this leaden state, you may well
become aware of the level of consciousness of the crystal;
extremely slow, extremely deliberate but none the less at
a very subtle level, still conscious. And as you are aware
of that level of consciousness of the crystal, you are also
aware that your own physical body is part of that same
level of consciousness. Because our body *is* made from
minerals, we are and have always been involved with the
mineral level of being, although because its rate of life
pulse is very low, we have tended to not notice it.

Give yourself plenty of time to get out of this meditation, as you begin to move your energy back upwards through your chakras until you are fully aligned within your body once again. It may feel that it is taking a great deal of time to get out of the dense feeling, and if it appears so to you, don't panic. What you are re-experiencing to a large degree is how your very first body felt— dense, leaden, and so difficult to move around that you may well have felt trapped inside it. This is the root of the 'trapped in the body' feelings that many people have.

The purpose of this chapter has been to put you in touch with various levels of your own Being, to give you a greater awareness of the multitude of life forces that are at work within you. In the next chapter, you will discover how those life forces relate to the flow of Life in the world around you, with some exercises to help you attune to that flow. As your own life is intimately linked with the rhythms of the earth itself, true healing cannot take place without becoming part of that rhythm.

5 Hearts and Flowers . . . and Trees

One of the most profound moments in my life, was literally a 'flash of insight', in which I realized that Life by its very nature, is rhythmic.

Life Pulses

As we open ourselves to deeper levels of our own Being, we also begin attuning ourselves to our own natural pulse of life. In doing so, we likewise begin to become aware of the pulse of all life around us. Many of you already have a high attunement to nature; it is perhaps through this attunement that many of you began to realize that your own life exists beyond the boundaries of your physical body.

All matter is in motion. Even the basic physical matter of your own body—its atoms and molecules—are always in motion. It has been found that atoms of hydrogen, contained in all body tissues, align in a certain direction if tissue is healthy, and in other directions if tissue is diseased. Even our atoms have some sort of 'awareness'.

There are even grounds in physics to suggest that rhythm is part of the biological memory of creation in *all* living organisms. One scientist has even presented the case in thermodynamic terms; that the flow of energy onto the earth from the sun is mathematically destined to bring matter into an increasingly ordered state.

The result is molecules of higher and higher complexity, with the emergence of cycles that regulate the storage and release of energy.

Rhythm in the organic kingdoms may well be the earliest memory—the score for the transformation of inanimate matter and chaos into the order of living things.

This seems to be programmed into the very cells of living organisms. They seem within themselves to preserve whatever sensory structures evolved in the very first single cell organisms, and to have retained them when cells began to gather together as colonies to form more complex organisms—such as your own body.

In Backster's work with plants, and even in scrapings from human tissue, polygraphs connected to even tiny bits of living tissue produced the same results—they responded to outside stimulae exactly the same way as whole organisms.[1]

Your own body certainly retains these sensory devices—whatever they might be. In bioenergetics the entire process is involved in unlocking cellular memory of past traumatic events, which causes muscles to 'freeze'.

Maintaining rhythm is absolutely essential to the survival of all organisms. Loss of rhythm in one part of an organism which is not quickly regained can upset the life process of the entire organism. Experiments have shown that artificially imposed rhythms, de-synchronization with a natural rhythm, is usually fatal.

In a classic experiment, regulatory glands from insects set to normal daytime were transplanted into other groups of the same insects, who were also on normal daytime—they all remained healthy.

When regulatory glands from those same insects whose day/night cycle was reversed were transplanted into normal insects, all of the insects whose cycles were abruptly reversed, died. In fact, most of them died from intestinal cancer.[2]

Much of our natural rhythm, both for ourselves and the plant and animal kingdoms, may be tied to the internal rhythms of the earth itself. These rhythms will be generated by the body of the earth—the mineral kingdom—and thus is totally related to the mineral nature of the earth. Our own lives are intimately connected through rhythm and cycle with the life of the planetary body itself.

The natural pulses in the earth's own magnetic and electrical fields, pulsing between 1 and 30 hz, and fluctuating every 24 hours, appear to set the internal clocks of most, if not all, organisms. They appear to affect hormone secretions in animals (and humans), that regulate sleep, etc.

[1] John Whitman, *The Psychic Power of Plants*, p. 32.
[2] John Whitman, p. 21.

In experiments, animal behaviour can be highly modified simply by changing the frequency of weak electromagnetic fields; these fields appear to alter brainwave function. Animals can be sent into a deep sleep, or into a frenzy, just by moving the frequency up and down.[3]

We know too that the human body is very sensitive to the earth's magnetic field—during sunspot cycles when the earth's magnetic field is disturbed, admissions to mental hospitals skyrocket!

We are only just beginning to understand the effect of electromagnetic fields on the human body. The first concrete discoveries were made in 1952 by a German scientist, Professor W.O. Schumann, who identified waves of very low frequency associated with the earth's own magnetic and electrical field.

These waves may well be generated between the inner and outer core of the earth. The outer core is molten, and therefore some 'slippage' occurs as the earth rotates, between the outer part of the earth and the inner core. This would have the effect of a dynamo, generating not only the magnetic field, but other energies as well. The total mineral make-up of the earth would have a great deal of effect on exactly which waves are generated.

Professor Schumann suggested that these waves may influence all life. In fact, it probably goes far beyond that—life as it evolved on the earth would have evolved in harmony with these waves. Any creatures attempting to evolve that were *not* in harmony with them, would have died out immediately.

Important evidence about the earth's wave effects came from some of the first manned space flights—flights at a distance from the earth where the wave effects were very much reduced. Astronauts returned feeling distressed and disorientated—until devices for generating Schumann waves were installed in the spacecraft. Schumann waves pulse almost within the same frequency as brainwaves—between 1 and 30 hz.

Jet lag may be a result of being shielded by the plane's metallic casing, and flying at an altitude where Schumann waves are considerably weaker. It is usually made worse by moving to a place where the waves are pulsing at a different

[3] Elizabeth Blair, 'Changing Wavelengths', *You*, Oct 18, 1987, p. 127.

point in their 24-hour rhythm. Stewardesses on long-haul duty often experience irregular periods, and may stop menstruating altogether.[4]

In my own experience of around the world travel, I have found that by placing a crystal in each pocket, on the right- and left-hand side of the body, and by intending to keep my body rhythms and energy flows in balance, jet lag is significantly reduced.

Dr Robert Moore of the University of California is convinced that the regulating mechanism of our internal body cycles is a tiny cluster of nerve cells, the Suprachiasmatic nucleus, located at the base of the brain. This is in the most primitive part of the brain, and is thus most linked to natural rhythms.

Our own human ability to experience pleasure seems to be directly related to an ability to flow with our own natural rhythms. In painful states, we lack co-ordination with our own rhythms; in a pleasurable state our movements are smooth and rhythmic.[5]

The very definition of pleasure in Dr Lowen's work is defined as '. . . the conscious perception of the rhythmic and pulsatory activity of the body'.

He also says:

> The feeling of pleasure that stems from a natural and undisturbed rhythm of life embraces all our activities and relationships. There is a time to work and a time to rest, a time to play and a time to be serious, a time to be together and a time to be alone. Too much togetherness can be as painful as too much aloneness, and too much playing can be as dull as too much work. *The rhythms that govern life are inherent in life*; they cannot be imposed from without. Each individual knows what his rhythms are and knows by the feelings of pain or lack of pleasure when his rhythms are disturbed.[6] (Emphasis in original)

In the book *The Naked Ape*, Desmond Morris notes that the pattern followed by humans in the establishment of their own natural routines is as follows:

---

[4] Ibid.
[5] Alexander Lowen, *Pleasure*, p. 238.
[6] Ibid.

1. You shall investigate the unfamiliar until it has become familiar;
2. You shall impose rhythmic repetition on the familiar;
3. You shall vary this repetition in as many ways as possible;
4. You shall select the most satisfying of these variations and develop these at the expense of others;
5. You shall combine and recombine these variations with one another.[7]

He further points out that these rules apply to every spectrum of human activity at all ages, from a child in a sandpit to a composer writing a symphony.

The sensitivity of plants and animals to natural rhythm can be demonstrated in two classic examples: it was shown that if dry grain seed was kept in a container at constant temperature, the percentage of seed taken from the container that will germinate depends on the season of the year. Dry seed kept at low temperature is almost always lifeless; how could the seed be aware of the season of the year when it is taken from the container?[8]

In the animal kingdom, an example is the bean aphid, which can either give birth to live offspring or lay eggs, depending on the time of the year and the length of the day. When daylight lasts longer than 14 hours and 55 minutes, the offspring is born alive. If the day is even a few minutes shorter, the offspring is born inside an egg that will hatch later. Somewhere in the female bean aphid's body is a *very* finely tuned mechanism.

Plants have been shown to be highly sensitive to rhythms that are imposed on them. In her book *The Sound of Music in Plants*, Dorothy Retallack recounts experiments in which she played various sorts of music to plants.

She discovered that classics and pop classic music stimulated plant growth, and created hearty plants with lush foliage. Plants that were played this music tended to grow toward the music source.

Rock music on the other hand, created plants growing in bizarre and grotesque shapes, which soon died. These plants tried to escape the music by growing away from the music

[7] Desmond Morris, *The Naked Ape*, p. 121.
[8] Michael Gauquelin, *The Cosmic Clocks*, p. 126.

source. In her experiments a number of different types of plants all responded in the same way. Other research has shown that random noise can retard the growth of plants by as much as 40 per cent.

A fascinating experiment was performed in India, where there has been a long tradition that sacred dances generate an energy that can be picked up by plants.

An Indian sacred dance was performed daily for a batch of marigolds. These plants grew 60 per cent taller than the control marigolds in an 'undanced' batch. The experimenter believes that the plants were responding to the rhythms of the dance transmitted through the ground.[9]

It has been observed that in polygraph (lie detector) tracings, plants tune into their masters by matching beat for beat, the pulsating heart of their owners.[10]

In other polygraph experiments, hooked-up plants were placed with groups of students talking about various subjects. When dull subjects such as engineering were being discussed, the tracings showed little activity. But when sex was discussed, the tracings became quite active![11]

Some of the pioneer scientific discoveries about interactions between plants and the human kingdom were made by Cleave Backster. On a purely whimsical thought he decided to hook a polygraph up to a plant in his office—after a while he noticed something fascinating; the plant was showing a tracing almost identical to that shown by humans who were experiencing somewhat mild emotional stimulation.

His next step was to see if a plant would show a similar response to humans experiencing fear and anxiety—an immediate polygraph response.

What he discovered was startling—he only had to *think* about burning the leaf with the electrode attached and the polygraph leapt into action, showing a pattern of anxiety.

Backster later discovered that plants respond immediately when certain people enter the room, and even showed a severe 'anxiety' reaction when one person whose job involved roasting plants entered the room.

He also demonstrated that plants can pick up anxiety signals from animals, even if they are in another room.[12]

[9] Dorothy Retallack, *The Sound of Music and Plants*, p. 60.
[10] John Whitman, p. 32.   [11] Ibid., p. 79.
[12] Ibid., p. 33.

A device was constructed to dump live brine shrimp (mostly used as tropical fish food), into a container of boiling water at random intervals. As a control, the machine would randomly dump water with no shrimp into boiling water.

The experiment was done with no one in the building to send any thoughts to the three philodendrons in separate rooms, each hooked up to its own polygraph. Each of the three showed acute stress symptoms each time shrimp was dumped, and no reaction at all when only water was dumped. Clearly, they were responding to the distress of the dying shrimp.

Plants have even been shown to have a sensitivity to minerals. Dr Victor Adamenko trained plants to respond in the presence of a specific mineral, and, in a significant number of experiments, they did just that.[13]

Recent experiments by a doctor in Australia have shown that the growth of salt crystals can be influenced by human thought, and that the crystals communicated their new growth patterns to each other once the new patterns were established, and that a pattern of distribution of these 'communications' followed a rhythmic pattern.

The purpose of all of the preceding is to demonstrate to you as briefly as possible that life is, by its nature, rhythmic, and that all levels of life exhibit a high degree of sensitivity to each other. As you begin to open yourself to your own deep inner self-awareness, you will begin to sensitize yourself not only to your own natural rhythms, but to the rhythms of the world around you.

In the following exercises, the process will be reversed: by deliberately sensitizing yourself to certain of the natural rhythms around you, you will be enabled to be more sensitive to your own rhythms.

As Dr Lowen has clearly shown, the healing process cannot take place without it.

[13] Cleave Backster, 'Evidence of Primary Reception in Plant Life', *International Journal of Parapsychology*, vol. X, 1968, no. 4, p. 330.

The Pulse of Earth

Purpose:
To attune yourself to the natural pulse and rhythm of
the Earth Being.

Crystal:
The crystal for this meditation is placed on the heart.
Choose a crystal that feels like it embodies the words
'The Earth'.

Programme:
To reflect back to you the pulse of your own life that is
in harmony with the natural pulse of the earth itself.

This meditation is done out of doors, and although it is
desirable to have your body in contact with the earth,
you will probably find that a blanket, especially one
made of a natural material such as cotton, will not affect
the intensity of the experience.

Lie with your head to the north and the crystal resting
over your heart. Take in several deep breaths and let
them out slowly, and then let your breathing go to
whatever pattern is natural for you at that moment.

As you breathe, feel as if you are breathing the soil
beneath you into your lungs and exhaling it. You will
soon find your breathing falling into a natural rhythm,
that may well be different from the one you just began.

Feel as if your body is melting into the earth, and that
you and the earth are one being. As you do this, you will
find that there is a very natural rhythm which seems to
come from the earth itself, but which also penetrates
and permeates your being.

Hug a Tree

Purpose:
You will not actually be hugging a tree in this exercise,
but it is designed to help you feel the natural pulse and

rhythm connected to the plant kingdom, through the symbol of a tree.

Crystal:
A crystal selected to reflect back to you the natural pulse and rhythm in the plant kingdom.

Programme:
To reflect to you the pulse of life expressed through the living essence of a tree.

Any tree will do for this exercise, although you need one where you can sit with your back to the trunk, and your spine as fully in contact with the trunk as possible. The crystal is placed over the heart. As you sit with your back to the tree, close your eyes and let your breathing fall into your own personal relaxed pattern.

Then, visualize yourself melting into the trunk of the tree, with the crystal staying 'outside' the tree. As you feel an increasing sense of oneness with the tree, you will begin to feel another pulse, another breath. This will be the pulse of the tree itself, and through that pulse you can begin to experience 'treeness'. The first time I did this exercise, I was suddenly aware of the sunlight on my leaves!

To complete the experience, visualize the crystal (which has stayed outside the tree), feel your own connection to that crystal, and let it feel as if it is 'pulling' you out of the tree.

When you are finished with this exercise, you may hug the tree!

6 Heart to Heart

For healing to take place in close relationships, especially one-to-one intimate relationships, it is necessary for healing to take place in yourself first. All relationships are just externalizations of your own inner relationship with yourself.

Your first love relationships were those with your parents, and, until that relationship becomes healed, you will keep acting those relationships out with each new partner. There are two excellent books on relationships listed in the Additional Reading section at the end of this book, and my own experience, both of myself, and as a counsellor, bear out exactly the things that are written in those books.

The most important point of the whole chapter is this: **Any issues that are unresolved with your parents, you will continue to act out in your close personal relationships**. You will create in those relationships exactly the same relationships that you had with your parents.

Now, this is good news and bad news: bad news from the standpoint that you will *never* have the sort of personal relationship you really want until you resolve your parent issues. But, the good news is that as you resolve your parent issues, *you also heal yourself*.

Most of the physical illness in our lives is a direct result of beliefs about ourselves, beliefs that limit the free flow of energy through our bodies. And in doing so, we limit who we are. These beliefs or ideas usually come from our parents and often take the form of **injunctions**. One such injunction is shown diagrammatically in Figure 7.

Here, the injunction 'be a good boy/girl' means that to be 'good', we have to do what someone else wants us to do. In this case it's our parents, and being 'good' may well mean sup-

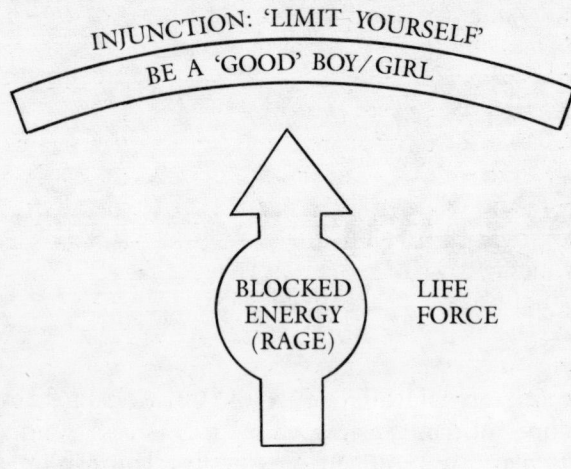

Figure 7

pressing our natural exuberance and joy, the natural childlike expressions of our life force. Our parents seldom inhibit us purposely; they will do so because their own life force is inhibited in some way, and seeing that life force have its full expression in a child brings up their own deep pain at their own repression. Therefore, in order to stop feeling their own pain, it is necessary for them to repress you. And, in repressing you as a child, because you are dependent on your parents for survival, not being 'good' appears to pose a direct threat to your physical survival. How can we not be 'good' (repressing our own life force) when the alternative appears to be death!

Because there is such a strong energetic barrier to the free flow of our life force, all that energy must be held somewhere in the body, or given expression in some other form. It can come out as compulsive behaviour, but eventually, because the energy is being mischannelled, it will come out as disease. So, our disease serves us—if we are willing to see, and re-experience, the events which created the repression in the first place. Our disease is like an arrow pointing directly to the source of our illness; our own self-limiting beliefs. The problem is in seeing it.

In most cases, there is a large sense of denial operating in the psyche. Because children need to see their parents as perfect (and if they weren't, what a threat to survival *that* would be!), children tend to deny that there is anything wrong, or take the blame for anything not right on themselves. By the time this mechanism of denial has been operating for many years it becomes second nature, unnoticed, even to the point where we deny we have denial!

It doesn't mean that these barriers cannot be worked through. But it does mean that there is a necessity for clear intention, and willingness to experience pain and discomfort, in order to work through these issues.

Dr John Harrison makes the point that if illness is to be cured, then 'some or all of the following need to happen: awareness ("So that's how I make myself ill!"), expression ('Damn you Mom!"), forgiveness ("I accept the burden that raising six kids in the Depression must have been") and acceptance ("I love me, and I love others"). This will ultimately mean dropping our old system of beliefs, and taking full responsibility for who we are.

I have spoken at length in this book about mirroring and reflection. At this point I need to emphasize again that the state of your body is a mirror of your beliefs about yourself; and your relationships with others are a reflection of the relationships you had with your parents, which, at the deepest level, are a further reflection of your relationships with yourself.

The use of crystals in this healing process is not merely a matter of waving them over yourself and your relationships like magic wands. Nothing is going to get fixed, until you fix yourself.

And in order to do so, you must begin to see yourself more clearly. Here fortunately we have an ally: the clear reflections of the crystal. In the following exercises, you will use those reflections to begin looking more deeply into yourself, focused around the subject of relationships. This will be a sticking point for some of you. Those who believe in instant anything are going to be disappointed. Unravelling the twisted threads of your own life is time-consuming and it takes a great deal of energy and dedication. And it will eventually require you to feel some uncomfortable feelings. Even the Buddha said words to the effect of: 'Your ability to achieve enlightenment is a direct result of your ability to endure pain.'

This does not mean, by the way, experiencing pain for the sake of pain, but rather experiencing those deep pains at the centre of each of us—all springing from the original pain of separating from our Source, and taking on a body. As we will see in Chapter 8, this was an illusory separation, but strong enough illusions take on the power of reality, at least as far as creating disease in the body is concerned. The body makes no judgements or discernments; everything is taken at face value, taken as it *appears* to be. This is largely because the energy patterns of the body are set in infancy and early childhood, before we have enough experience of the world to make judgements and discernments. And, because these decisions about life take place at the very deepest level of our physical being, the primitive brain and the primitive body (at least emotionally), they are connected with our most primal fears, and, because they are primal, underlie everything that our personality has later built on top of it. In fact, it is these primal fears that *create* and give form to all of the later developments of the ego and personality.

In the following processes you will begin to discover what some of your self-limiting beliefs are, where they came from, and move toward the forgiveness that is your only true release from them.

In the following exercise, you can begin to search your own experience for those injunctions which have limited your life. The first exercise is in looking at some of the clichés and sayings that were common in your family. As children, we often take these very literally (take them to heart). You will want your notebook and pen close at hand, and you may find it necessary to write some of these down with your eyes closed, so that you don't miss any of them—some of them may flash past very quickly. In the exercise, look for any stereotype situations, and the stereotype remarks that either of your parents would have made. Or any sort of sayings that your parents continually repeated: for example: 'money is the root of all evil'. Such a saying taken literally would certainly cause us to limit our ability to make money, for, after all, who wants to be evil!

Injunctions 1

Purpose:
To uncover family sayings and beliefs that may have shaped your beliefs about yourself as a child.

Crystal:
For this exercise, use crystals on both the brow and the heart. This exercise involves memory of those sayings that you have 'taken to heart'.

Programme:
To reflect back to you ideas and beliefs, especially clichés, that have shaped your self-image.

Allow yourself to remember a pleasant time as a child, to remember how it felt to be that child. As you feel being the child, feel the presence of your parents around you. Go first to whatever age you intuitively sense you picked up the strongest injunctions. It is possible that there are others that are even deeper and stronger, and as you repeat this exercise at later times, others may come to the surface. For now, though, go to a particular age when one of these sayings stuck.

If you are not able to go to a particular age, then you may well remember these injunctions by completing the following sentences: Daddy/Mummy (use whatever terms here you actually called them by as a child) always used to say: '————.' Or, you might remember particular situations when Daddy/Mummy could always be counted on to say: '————.' As you recall these sayings, be particularly aware of your body sensations, and if you experience any sort of body distress, move the energy into the heart using the Shifting Energy to the Heart exercise.

When you have completed the exercise, make a list in your notebook of the various injunctions, and note for each injunction that you remember, what your experience of it was—what was your understanding of its meaning as a child, and how has that affected the way you see your life now.

Injunctions 2

Purpose:
The purpose of this exercise is to uncover the more subtle injunctions, some of which may have been unspoken. You will probably wish to do this exercise a number of times, as you are likely to uncover quite a large number of them.

Crystal:
A crystal on the brow, and on the heart, chosen for their sense of subtle reflection.

Programme:
To reflect back to you the subtle injunctions that have been self-limiting.

This exercise can be done sitting or lying down, although you may find it more powerful sitting, with the feet firmly on the ground, and the spine (chakras) vertical.

There are an enormous number of early life situations that can be examined here, and you will probably wish to repeat this exercise a number of times.

In this exercise we will be looking for life-limiting injunctions that are subtle or implied. For example, what did it mean in your home when you were told 'be a good boy/girl'? Almost always this answer will involve a list of things that you *did* do, and a possibly longer list of things that you *didn't* do. As you remember each of these things, try to feel in your heart the subtle nuances of them. For example, as you began to exhibit more and more independence, did your parents assert strong pressures to control you? A subtle message from this could be 'stay a dependent child'.

Or, perhaps you overheard a remark your mother or father made to a friend: 'he is such a sickly child'. The injunction from this one would be: 'be sick!'

Most of the injunctions you have discovered will be incorporated in the part of your psyche that is often referred to as the Parent Self.

This is one of the three ego states that make up every human being. An ego state is a system of feelings accompanied by a related set of behaviour patterns. When you are in your Parent state, you are actually in the same state of mind as one of your parents (or a parent substitute) once was, and you are responding as he would, with the same posture, gestures, vocabulary, and feelings.

There are two other ego states: the Adult and the Child. The Adult is the part of you that makes objective appraisals of situations, acts without prejudice, and frequently serves as a mediator between the parent and child states.

And, the Child state, where the manner and intent of your reaction is just as it would be if you were a little boy or little girl.

Everyone, including children and the mentally retarded, have all three of these states functioning to varying degrees. These three aspects of the personality are often segregated from each other, and are often quite inconsistent, or directly in conflict with each other.

Each of these states is useful and necessary, and it is only when they are out of balance with each other that the whole being is out of balance. The conflicts which arise, especially between the Parent and Child ego states, create enormous stresses in the body, and are frequently the source of much illness. Another way of looking at it, is that *illness is a way our body draws attention to the imbalance in our ego states*.

There is an odd notion among many 'spiritual' people, that the ego is something to be eliminated or decommissioned. The ego is a perfectly normal and healthy part of the existence of every Being on the earth, and it is the structure through which our learning about living on the earth takes place. Any attempt to decommission the ego is ultimately futile, as you are attempting to decommission the very learning mechanism that you came here for in the first place! All three of the ego states are necessary, useful, and totally desirable. It is only when they are out of balance that problems occur. For example, when the Child received little acknowledgement by recognition of himself as a child, he will often go to extremes to get that recognition when he grows up. In order to defend the wounded part of himself, he will become 'egotistical' seeking to fill in the emptiness. There is nothing 'wrong' with this person—he is merely acting out his need to reharmonize himself, until he can recognize his reflection in the outer world, the responses of others to his imbalanced state. Most energy goes in trying to meet the needs of the inner Child. Any of our needs that were unmet in our own childhood we will continually strive to get met through the remainder of our lives. But, there is a problem.

Because we are reliant on our inner Parent to meet those needs, we are mostly doomed to fail. Because our inner Parent has learnt to be a parent from our actual parents, and *we parent ourselves as our parents parented us!* Where your parents failed to meet your needs, so your inner Parent will fail also.

The function of the inner Parent is to create a system of automatic responses so that your Adult doesn't spend an enormous amount of energy reasoning out trivial or repetitive situations—for example: it is your inner Parent who says 'look both ways before you cross the street'. It is therefore unnecessary for your Adult to reason out the necessity for doing so each time; all that your Adult has to do is compute the automobiles that are on the street, and compute your probability of safely reaching the other side.

We also attract partners whose Parent selves are exactly like our own parents. So, our partners aren't able to meet our unfulfilled needs either!

All people have a complete, well-structured Adult self that only needs to be activated or uncovered. People who are 'immature' are only people in whom the Child takes over inappropriately. Likewise, 'mature' people are those in whom the Adult is in control, often inappropriately, and in whom the Child will take over on occasion (such as when large amounts of alcohol have been consumed), often with unproductive results.

There is much pleasure to be obtained from the Adult state, and it usually comes in the form of activities where computation is successful, such as planning the outcome of a business activity, budgeting your incomes successfully, card games where skill with reasoning is essential, flying, sailing, and other types of mobile sports, and so forth. Another major task of the Adult is to regulate the activities of the Parent and Child and mediate between them when conflicts arise. If the Adult has not been uncovered or fully activated, the internal battle that can take place between the Parent and Child can consume enormous amounts of energy, and severely limit the productivity of the life of the person involved.

Clearly, sorting our parent-child conflicts must be a major concern in the growing process.

I have left the discussion of the Child self until last, as in many ways the Child can be the most valuable part of the personality: the Child contributes charm, pleasure and creativity. If the Child is confused and unhealthy, constantly seeking what was unfulfilled in its own childhood, then the balance of the entire individual is upset.

It is important to distinguish the word Child from the word 'Childish'. A person who is 'childish' is simply a person whose Child takes over at inappropriate times. The reflection in the world of this state is the need to fulfil the unmet needs of the inner Child.

There is the natural Child within us, the state of innocence and openness in which we were born, and there is the adapted Child who has had to modify his behaviour under Parental influence. His behaviour is as his parents wanted him to behave: behaviour often dictated by the imbalances in the parents' own lives.

The result of this, is that the child closes off part of his being, his heart, in order to survive in an environment that is not natural to his own state of Being. Thus, working with and healing the heart centre of necessity involves seeking out the imbalances in the inner Parent/Child relationship.

To emphasize once again: all three aspects of the personality have a good survival and living value, and it is only when one or the other of them disturbs the healthy balance that there is a necessity for inner corrections to be made.

The good news about all of this is that it *is* possible to make these corrections. All of the behaviour of the Parent and the adapted Child is learned behaviour and it ultimately becomes a matter of re-educating both aspects of the Self. This is where the power of the Adult comes into play. Because our inner Parent fails to meet the need of our inner Child as our parents failed to meet our needs, that role can be taken over for a time by our own Adult. And, as our Adult is meeting the needs of our inner Child, so can we also begin re-educating our inner Parent so that we can begin parenting ourselves as we had always wanted our parents to parent us. Our Child knows what it wants and needs, and for some reason our natural parents were unable to fulfil those needs. As we discover the inadequacies in our internal Parents, we can also gain the deeper understanding of our natural parents, thus opening the door to forgiveness.

The reason all of this exists in the first place, is that *these are the lessons that you have chosen to work through in this particular lifetime.* You have chosen the parents that you did, in order that they would fail you in appropriate ways, to make certain you learned the lessons you are learning. All parents fail. If they didn't, you would have nothing to learn.

The initial stage of the healing process, then, involves identifying the three different parts of the Self, and then beginning to work constructively with those parts to firstly meet the needs of the inner Child, and secondly to re-educate the Parent self, so that you can begin fully meeting your own needs.

As discussed later, one of the main reasons we create relationships is to meet the needs of our inner Child. But, because you always attract partners who have Parent selves like your own Parent self, they are never able to meet those needs either. Your partners are there as mirrors, so that you can begin to see, understand, and forgive your own parents.

In the following exercises, you will use the reflective powers of crystals to reflect back to you these aspects of yourself, and allow you to begin working constructively with them, for self-healing.

Discovering the Child Self

Purpose:
The purpose of this exercise is to identify the Child self, and to begin a dialogue between the Child self and the Adult self, leading to fulfilment of the needs of the Child.

Crystals:
Two crystals are used for this exercise: a crystal to reflect back to you the Child self, and a crystal to reflect back to you the Adult self. The crystals are placed as described in the exercise.

Programme:
One crystal is programmed to reflect back your Child self and the second to reflect back your Adult self.

This exercise takes no note of the Parent self, as this is purely to identify the Adult and the Child selves, and begin a dialogue between those two aspects of the self, allowing the Adult to fulfil the needs of the Child that the Parent self is unable to do.

The exercise is done using two chairs, and two crystals. The two chairs should be placed side by side, so it is easy to move from one chair to the next with your eyes closed.

The Adult crystal should be placed on one chair, and the Child crystal should be placed on the second chair.

To begin the exercise, sit in the Adult chair, holding the Adult crystal in your hands. Close your eyes, and allow the feeling to come over you that you have when you *know* that you are in a fully Adult state. That is, totally clear, totally non-judgemental, totally non-emotional. It doesn't matter whether or not you have spent any amount of time in this state; just allow it to be reflected back to you, whether it is well developed or not. Then, imagine that you are going to leave that Adult person sitting in that chair, and physically move your body to the second chair, leaving the Adult crystal on the first chair. Do this with your eyes closed, as it helps to sustain the visualization. When you are in the Child chair, hold the Child crystal in your hand, and go back to a time in your childhood when you felt very upset by something your parents (either one will do) had done. If there are many such occasions, choose the one which brings up the worst feelings in the body as you sit in the chair.

The deeper you go into these feelings, the more you will be in a childlike state. If someone were to speak to you at this time, you would answer with childlike phrases and possibly even in a childlike voice. You may not accomplish this fully on the first attempt, but the more you practise this exercise, the more you will *become* a child in the exercise.

When you are in your Child state, then become aware of the Adult sitting next to you. Know that that Adult is capable of fulfilling whatever need you have in that moment as a child. If you are in pain or distress, what action could that Adult take to help you feel better, to make the pain go away? A cuddle? Words of reassurance? Whatever your need is in that moment that would make you feel better, then simply allow your Adult to fulfil that need.

If the need is for a cuddle for example, then just visualize and feel that Adult in the chair next to you putting their arms around you, and holding you in whatever way you would like to be held. If the need is for reassurance, then let your Adult speak the words to you that you would most like to hear. And so on.

If you are working with a partner in this exercise, then the partner can ask you the questions about what you are feeling, and what you would like your Adult to do to relieve that feeling. But, it is **not recommended** that your partner act out the role of Adult. The object of this exercise is to fulfil your *own* needs, without the need to resort to external sources. In doing so, you will energetically clean up your own inner relationship which will be reflected outwardly in more fulfilling outer relationships.

When your Child has had its needs met by the Adult, then physically move back into the Adult chair, and allow the Adult part to be reabsorbed by your body. When you feel integrated, then do some deep breathing and open your eyes.

When you have done this exercise a number of times, you can dispense with the chairs entirely, and do the exercise sitting on the edge of a bed, or perhaps on a couch. Anywhere where it is possible to make a physical movement of your body. As you become more and more proficient with these two roles, you will eventually find it unnecessary to move the body at all, as you will be able to identify from certain body feelings which part of you is the Child, and which part of you is the Adult. Both of these states will have different body sensations, and as you do this exercise in the chairs you will eventually begin to notice that you feel different physically when you are in each of these ego states. I recommend becoming thoroughly proficient with this exercise before going on to the next one, which brings in the Parent role.

In the following exercise, the Parent is identified, and the Adult acts in the role of mediator between the Parent and the Child. It is in this exercise that many of the conflicts between the Parent self and the Child self will emerge. I found in my own experience of this exercise that my Child was very spiteful and angry, and was punishing the Parent self at every available opportunity, as if the Parent self were the real parent. This took the form of my own Child undermining my financial successes. Money was always a major issue in my home as a child, and as a child I felt that money was more important than love. Once I had identified that conflict, then I allowed my Adult to explain to my Child the self-defeating nature of this conflict, and as my Child began to receive the love it wanted from my Adult, there was less and less need for the Child to undermine and punish. And as a result, my financial life is constantly improving!

A variation on the last exercise is for you to begin the exercise in the Child chair, and then move to the Adult chair. Then, visualize seeing your needy Child in the other chair, and experience yourself as an Adult fulfilling the needs of that Child.

Identifying the Parent

Purpose:
To identify the Parent self, and begin a dialogue between the Parent and the Child, in order to identify areas of inner conflict.

Crystals:
You need three crystals for this exercise, one for the Parent, one for the Adult and one for the Child, placed as per the directions.

Programme:
Each of the three crystals is programmed to reflect back to you that particular part of yourself; the Parent, the Adult and the Child.

This exercise is done using three chairs, one for the Parent, one for the Adult, and one for the Child, with the appropriate crystal placed on each chair, with the Adult chair in the middle, and the Child chair in the same position as the Child chair in the previous exercise.

Begin this exercise sitting in the Child chair, identify the Child self, then move to the Adult chair leaving the Child crystal in the Child chair; as in the previous exercise make this physical movement with your eyes closed.

When you are in the Adult chair, identify the Adult feelings, then, with your eyes still closed, and leaving the Adult crystal on the Adult chair, move into the Parent chair, and pick up and hold in your hand the Parent crystal.

Take a couple of minutes to visualize seeing the Adult you sitting in the middle chair, and the Child you sitting in the Child chair. See the Child you as you actually looked as a child. As you sit in the Parent chair, you may begin to notice different body feelings and senstions, feelings and sensations that are distinctly different from those you experienced in the other two chairs.

When you feel some sort of identity with the Parent self, then see if there is anything you would like to say to your Child, and do so. Do this out loud if possible, verbalizing to the Child any feelings, thoughts, or anything else that comes to mind you would like to say to the Child.

If your Child is particularly angry, you may well experience your Child saying something back to you in return. Should any sense of conflict begin developing between your Parent self and your Child self, then leave your Parent sitting in the Parent chair, and physically move back into the Adult chair. Then, in your Adult state, you can become the mediator of the conflict, and, in this state, you may need to offer explanations to both the Parent and the Child for the point of view of each other.

For example, if your Parent should say to your Child: 'I am sorry I don't give you more time,' your Child might come back with something like 'You don't really love me.'

The Adult as mediator might then explain to the Child that sometimes parents have other responsibilities, such as earning a living, and are not always able to give the child what it wants in the moment, and that this does not mean that the child is unloved; in fact, it may mean just the opposite, that the parent's way of expressing love to the child was to work hard in order to provide the child with adequate food and shelter. This may not be the kind of love that the child *wanted*, but it none the less *was* love. Children are remarkably open to reason, and you will probably find this sort of an explanation is readily accepted by your Child, or at least a new state of realization will dawn for the Child. In the real-life situation, this was probably true; the parents didn't give the child enough time, but they were, in their own way, giving the child love, although they never bothered to explain it to the child (or even recognized a need to do so).

The next stage for the Adult would be to turn to the Parent and explain that although they are giving the Child love in their way, the Child is unable to see it that way, and that the child's *real* need is for more time.

There is nothing wrong whatsoever with acting out these activities in your own life; when you have finished the exercise, let your Parent self take your Child self out for an ice cream! In fact, wherever possible, I encourage acting out (in a healthy way of course) any of these activities which fulfil the Child part of yourself. You will find that in your own life, you have actually denied yourself the very things which your parents denied you.

There are an infinite number of variations on the Parent/Child conflict, but all of them will revolve around the Child not getting some real or perceived need met. Often the Parent will feel unjustly accused, and it is in the Adult's capacity for dispassionately seeing the situation as it really is that the Parent can be re-educated to see the needs of the Child are met, and the Child can be re-educated to see that his realistic needs are met, and likewise to see when his needs are unrealistic.

When you have completed this exercise, draw all three of the selves back together, take a few deep breaths, and come back fully into your body.

The result of this exercise will eventually be that you can identify the part of yourself that is the Parent without having to physically move: that there are certain body sensations that are associated with that state of being. And likewise, that there are certain ways of thinking, ways of speaking, and more or less stereotyped injunctions that you give to yourself, that will all be coming from your Parent.

Another benefit of identifying the Parent self, and perhaps the greatest benefit of all, is that you can open the door to your own understanding of why your parents did what they did. As you begin to do this, you can move in to the next stage of relationship with your parents: forgiveness. Most of us carry around an enormous amount of anger at our parents, both for real and imagined inadequacies. Because we felt a need to limit ourselves to survive, our life force was blocked, creating rage. This is a good time to re-read the supplementary techniques for dealing with rage. Identifying those and beginning to resolve them is the result of the last exercise; in the next exercise, you can begin now to move to a deeper understanding of the problems that your parents had, and why it was that they failed you.

Understanding your Parents

Purpose:
To identify the Mother and Father aspects of your Parent self in enough depth to be able to see and understand their own problems and limitations, especially those that deeply affected you as a child.

Crystals:
A crystal for the Mother self, the Father self, and the Adult self.

Programme:
Each crystal is programmed to reflect back to you the appropriate aspect of the Parent self; the Mother self the Father self; and the Adult self.

This exercise is done with three chairs and three crystals, as in the previous exercise. The Father chair should be placed to the right of the Adult chair as you are sitting in it and the Mother chair to the left of the Adult chair. This also identifies with the male and female sides of the body, and provides less body confusion when you are switching roles.

Begin the exercise by sitting in the Adult chair, and remembering some particularly painful incident, or series of incidents for which you 'blamed' your parents. Try to find one each for your father and mother.

Since this is done in the Adult state, you will be discussing these events with your parents on an Adult-to-Adult basis, and therefore having identified by now the Child self, you as an Adult should request your inner Child to remain quiet and not get involved. You can do this by visualizing the small child inside you, and speaking directly to that Child as if the Child were actually present within your body.

Then leave your Adult sitting in the centre chair, and move into the chair of the Parent with whom you had the first identified difficulty. Pick up and hold the parent crystal, and visualize your own body transforming into the physical body of that particular parent. When you have done this exercise a few times you will actually feel yourself *becoming* that parent. Then, visualize your Adult asking you as your parent whatever questions you would always have liked to have asked that parent about that incident. You might also have your Adult ask that parent why they behaved as they did in that situation, and what were their own fears and perceived limitations in dealing with it. If not at first, then eventually, you will find yourself answering as if you actually *were* that parent.

When you have completed the exercise with the first parent, return that crystal to that chair, move back into the Adult, pick up the Adult crystal and re-identify yourself with that Adult state, then, placing the crystal back on the chair, move into the second parent, repeating the procedures as with the first one.

If you have issues with one parent much more than the other, this exercise can be done with only that parent with whom you have a need to deal in the moment, although it is a good idea to use the third chair and third crystal to separate out the parent that is not involved from the one that is.

At the end of this exercise move back into the Adult chair, and reintegrate as in the previous exercises.

From these exercises you can now begin to identify the aspects of your Parent self that come from your father and those that come from your mother. And you should begin gaining a deeper insight into their own limitations as parents, which were a direct result of their own fears, more than likely passed on from *their* parents.

This series of exercises involving your parents are some of the most important in the book, as it is your parents who created the learning situations that you have chosen to work through in this lifetime. You have chosen this set of parents because they will fail you in certain ways; ways which will set up for you the lessons you have chosen to learn. As one of the major lessons in living on the earth is forgiveness, beyond needing to release your anger and resentment at them anyway, the forgiveness lesson comes almost as a by-product. And, until you forgive your parents fully, which can ultimately only come through understanding, you will continue to project the same failures and resentments into your other relationships. All of these unresolved angers and resentments create energetic links which bind you, and the tie-cutting exercise can be used for dissolving these unhealthy ties. And the completion of these can be done through the Forgiveness exercises in Chapter 7.

I mentioned earlier that physical illness is a way in which our body demonstrates to us our need to re-examine our inner beliefs. The body is closely identified with the Child, and therefore any unresolved issues or any unmet needs involving the Child will be reflected in the body. This can take the form of physical illness, or it can even take the form of injury to the body. For example: my deepest unresolved issues are with my father, and 90 per cent of the injuries to my body have been to the right, masculine, side.

An exercise for quickly identifying whether your main issues are with your father or your mother can be done with a mirror. Sit in a comfortable position where you can see your face in the mirror, then cover the left side of your face with a sheet of paper. You will then be seeing the right side of your face in the mirror. How old is the face that you are seeing? Is it the face of an adult or the face of a child? If it is a child's face, how old is the child?

Then, repeat the exercise with the right side of the face. Do the left and right sides of your face look the same? If not, what is the difference? Is one side angry and the other side sad? What is the *quality* of the difference between the two?

If one side of your face is a great deal younger than the other, then there is a good indication that that is the side where you are the most stuck. If it is the left side that is younger, then something about your feminine side has failed to develop; the issue therefore is most likely with your mother. And vice versa the other side.

This is slightly complicated if you grew up in a home where the mother was masculine and the father was effeminate. It may well be that your masculine traits therefore came from your mother, and your feminine traits from your father. In experiencing both of your parents through the various exercises of this book, you will readily come to a realization of whether this is true or not. If it is, considerable confusion may exist within you in regard to your relationship to your opposite sex parent. The use of the exercises can begin to resolve that confusion, which may be exhibited in facial development as parent reversal; the masculine side of the face being frozen in childhood may reflect a mother issue, rather than a father one.

In the following exercise, you can begin to look at your unmet childhood needs, which may result in specific body malfunctions, either through illness or accident, and begin to identify the thoughts and beliefs that created them.

Roots of Illness

Purpose:
To identify specific ideas and beliefs that are associated with any specific illness or injury that you have.

Crystal:
A crystal to reflect back to you any specific imbalance in your body energies and to connect that imbalance to a specific idea or belief.

Programme:
To reflect back to you the idea or belief that is at the root of a specific ailment.

Lie on your back for this exercise. The crystal will be placed on the specific body area where a symptom is occurring; if you have had an injury to a specific body part, then place the crystal on that area. If you have an illness that involves a particular area of the body, place the crystal on that location.

Allow your full awareness to flow into the crystal, and, as you do so, you will find certain body feelings and sensations in that particular place.

Allow yourself to go into your own Child ego state, setting aside the Parent and Adult. As you are in the Child state, allow the feelings that are associated with the crystal to associate themselves with a specific childhood or infancy event.

There are several questions to ask your Child at this stage, and these questions can be asked by the Adult who is sitting alongside observing the proceedings. The questions are: When did I first experience these feelings or sensations? What event was associated with them? What belief do I have about myself as a result of this experience? And finally, why have I given myself this illness?

When you have discovered answers to these questions, then your Adult can ask your Child: what actions can I take to relieve the underlying feelings that are creating this illness? And, what change in my beliefs about myself or the state of the world need to be changed to release this illness?

When you have answers to these questions, you can use other techniques in this book to begin releasing the beliefs and feelings, and fulfilling the unfulfilled needs that create this need for illness. Use the tie-cutting technique for releasing beliefs and ideas about yourself, and use the Adult/Child technique for fulfilling your own unfulfilled needs.

While you are in the Child state, you may also be aware that some of the illnesses you have are directly connected to illness and beliefs that your parents have. Also, you may be aware in the Child state, that your parents made certain statements about their health, or about your health, that are energetically affecting your body. Some of these may have turned up in the Injunctions exercise, but some of them may also appear in this exercise. Use the tie-cutting exercise to begin releasing your attachment to these beliefs.

7 The Forgiving Heart

It is said that One Swallow doesn't make a Spring—nor does one experience make an inner opening. The opening processes, whatever they may be, will have to be repeated time and time again, but each time the heart becomes a little softer, a little more open to openness. In this chapter there are more exercises to free the heart, to release it from deeply held negative attachments, and move into a higher level of forgiveness. Indeed, it could be said that forgiveness is nothing more than releasing our unhealthy attachments to others; attachments of anger, hatred, resentment, and so forth.

It is also a process of moving out of the mind and more into the heart. And, moving more out of the lower emotional centres and into the heart.

Many of your unresolved emotional experiences are locked up in the lower energy centres, in energy at a very coarse level. As you move that energy into the heart where it can be processed through your own innate capacity for unconditional love, that energy is transmuted, and you gain a whole new perspective of the processes and events which generated them. There is less blaming of the people involved, and you are open to a new range of feelings for them. In his book *The I that is We*, Moss likens the process to transmuting the coarser energy of a waterfall into electricity. All emotional states are relative; shift the level of energy and the entire quality of the experience changes.

There are risks to be taken here of course. You will have to give up some favourite, and perhaps even addictive, feelings: anger, possessiveness, righteousness, self-importance, etc. And in doing so, open yourself to a whole new spectrum, feelings that are unfamiliar, and therefore feel threatening.

What you are moving toward is a state of unconditional love.

> Unconditional love is the embracing of all experience and the bringing of all the varying intensities to the level of the heart. At the heart level, unconditional love, which is an alive, vibrant, valueless state of awareness, replaces the varying intensities of mood and uncontrolled emotion and lifts the energy of these states into a finer, more radiant quality.[1]

As you shift into the heart more and more, you can begin to deal with issues without seeing them as absolutes. And therein, you can extract the maximum learning from them.

What this will move you into in your relationships with others, and internally in your relationships with yourself, is higher and higher states of understanding. And, as mentioned earlier, understanding is the first step toward forgiveness.

As you let go of all of the negative attachments, it frees an enormous amount of vital energy. But, unless you have managed a perceptual shift along the way, all of that vital energy will simply go back into the old patterns: relating to people and events, rather than the lessons that unfold from them.

Indeed, these sort of shifts are happening with many people, and yet so much of that vital energy goes into channels that are ultimately non-productive. The classic example of this is the shift that takes place through a peak experience of a flash of 'religious' insight. The vital energy that is freed from that shift is then put into religious fervour, into that person's limited concept of spirituality. It is as if they are confined in a narrow box, and suddenly an enormous amount of energy becomes available. But, rather than use the energy to break down the walls of the box and free themselves the energy goes into cramming themselves even more tightly into the box; without the perceptual shift, they don't even know they are in the box!

Herein lie the risks then. Truly, there is no way for you to fully anticipate who you might become through the awakening process. You can only discover it by becoming it. There are many clues along the way, however, so it is not a totally blind process. The exercises in the earlier portion of this book are designed to do just that: to give you a glimmer of

[1] Richard Moss, p. 22.

who you might be as a fully realized human being.

The following exercises are designed to set these processes firmly in motion. The first two of these are about cutting the unhealthy ties that you have to people, places, things, and ideas. This is a continuation of the earlier exercise of Clearing the Heart, and brings that clearing into a more focused level. Through many of the other exercises you will have discovered, especially in relation to your parents, that there are many attachments to them of anger, resentment, rage, and so forth. The following two exercises are a good place to begin specifically clearing those attachments. You have begun shifting them at one level using the Parent-Adult-Child exercises. Now, we can move into the deeper and more subtle levels of connection.

Cutting the Ties that Bind   1

Purpose:
This exercise is about cutting inappropriate attachments to people in our lives, or who have been in our lives.

Crystals:
A crystal on the brow and heart, chosen for a feeling of deep self-reflection.

Programme:
To reflect back to you any connections to other people that are not coming from a clear space in the heart, and that are therefore not serving the highest good of you or the other person involved.

As in previous exercises, you will go into the heart crystal, which is reflecting back to you your own heart centre. When you are inside the heart crystal, see it once again as a room, with the faces of the crystal as the walls of the room. Find a comfortable chair inside your crystal room, with its back against one of the walls.

Sitting opposite you will be an empty chair, and to the right a doorway entering into the crystal from outside.

Alongside your chair is a tool box and a pot of healing balm.

Summon into your crystal, the person with whom you wish to clear the inappropriate ties or attachments. Have them walk in through the door, and sit in the chair opposite you. Then, visualize any attachments that exist between you and that person, especially noticing where the attachments connect their body to your body. These attachments will be seen symbolically—perhaps as cables or cords, or steel bars, or perhaps even just as lines of energy. Then, reach into the tool-box alongside your chair, and pull out an appropriate tool for cutting those ties. When you have finished cutting them from yourself, offer the cutting tool to the person sitting in the chair opposite. They may or may not wish to take it and cut the ties themselves, but if they do not, it is of no consequence to you, as you are free to cut inappropriate ties any time you choose. If the person has chosen to cut away the ties from their side, then when they are finished, have them hand the tool back to you, and replace it in the tool box.

Then, go down your own body and pull out the roots of the ties which you have just cut loose. The energetic roots may go entirely through your body, so do whatever is necessary to pull them completely out. The person sitting in the chair opposite you may wish to do the same, if they have chosen to cut the ties themselves.

Then, see the ties that have been cut and the roots that have been pulled loose, lying on the floor between you. Reach into the tool box now, and select some appropriate means of disposing of the ties that have been cut loose. You may find a box of matches if the ties were something flammable, or if they were steel bars, you may find a laser to disintegrate them; but whatever method you choose, the bits that have been cut loose and pulled out should be totally destroyed.

After the process of destroying the connections has been completed, then reach to the other side of the chair and pick up the pot of healing balm and smoothe it over and into all of the places where the roots of your ties have been pulled from your body. When you have completed that, offer the pot to the other person so that they can complete healing themselves also. When they have completed whatever healing they wish, return the pot to its position alongside the chair.

When this healing process has been completed, if you wish to do so, you can now visualize and reinforce any appropriate ties that you have to that person. Or, if this is completing a past relationship and you wish to release this person energetically from your life, then visualize them slowly fading away even as they sit in the chair opposite, until they have completely disappeared.

If this is a person that you do not wish to see again in this lifetime, but wish to meet in another lifetime, then before you see that person fade away from the chair, attach a thread of gold from your heart to theirs, a thread that will draw you together again in another life-time.

If it is a relationship that you wish to maintain and continue in this lifetime, then simply see the person get up from the chair, and walk out of the door.

There is no limit to the number of people you can call into your crystal each time you do the exercise, but it is best in all instances to have them come into the crystal one at a time, so there is clarity about the ties that are being cut or reinforced.

When you have completed the exercise, then, as before, see the crystal beginning to shrink as you begin to get larger, until you pop outside the crystal and you and the crystal both return to your normal respective sizes.

After the exercise, write in your notebook the exact nature and feeling of the ties that you cut, where they were connected to the other person, and the responses of the other person throughout the exercise. And, of course, any thoughts or feelings that you had as you were doing the exercise.

The next exercise is for clearing out any ideas or beliefs that are self-limiting, or any unhealthy attachments to places or things.

These ideas may have appeared in the other exercises: 'I am

a bad boy/girl'; 'I am unloveable'; 'I hurt my mother when I was a child'; etc., etc.

Or, 'I'll never have enough money, love, etc., etc.'; 'I can't survive if I lose my house, car, etc.'

Cutting the Ties   2

Purpose:
This exercise is for cutting ties to places, things, and ideas that are in any way self-limiting.

Crystal:
A crystal for the brow and the heart, chosen for their feeling of connection to your own inner clarity.

Programme:
To reflect back to you any inappropriate and self-limiting ties to ideas, places, and things.

As in the previous tie-cutting exercise, go into the heart crystal, and once again find yourself seated in a chair with a tool box on one side of the chair and a pot of healing balm on the other side. This time, instead of a chair sitting opposite you, there will be a pedestal. On this pedestal you will place some object that is symbolic of an idea or of a place. Or if you were cutting a tie to an actual thing, such as a particular car or house, place the actual object on the pedestal.

As in the previous exercise, see any inappropriate attachments you have to that idea, place, or thing.

This is the place to start cutting ties to the self-limiting beliefs and injunctions that have turned up in the previous exercises. For example, if you have a self-limiting belief that says: 'I am always sick', then see yourself sitting on the pedestal in a state of wretched illness. Then, see what attachments you have to that belief. Again, this may take the form of lines, cables, bars of iron, or whatever.

Again, reach into your tool box and select an appropriate tool for cutting the tie. When the tie has been cut, it will drop to the floor in front of you, breaking its attachment to the idea, place, or thing as you cut it loose from your own body. When all of the ties have been cut, you will see the idea, place or thing fade away and disappear from the top of the pedestal. After it has faded away, pull from your body the roots of the attachments, and add them to the rest of the cut-loose attachments that are lying on the floor. Then, reach into your tool kit and extract the appropriate means of destroying the attachments; matches, a blow torch, a laser, etc.

When you have thoroughly destroyed all of the pieces you have cut free, return the destroying implement to the tool box. Then, pick up the pot of healing balm and use it to fill in the places where the roots were pulled loose from your body.

When you have completed the exercise, then come out of the crystal as in the previous exercise.

The previous tie-cutting exercises can be used in your relationships with anyone. With your parents, with your spouses or lovers. To emphasize again: they are not necessarily to rid your life of someone, although you can use them for that if you wish; they are for cutting unhealthy attachments, and reinforcing healthy ones.

As you clear the heart of its old and inappropriate attachments, and as the corresponding energetic shifts begin to happen, your own capacity to process your coarser emotions through the heart increases also, as previously mentioned. In the following exercise, you can begin to consciously develop your capacity for this.

Shifting Energy to the Heart

Purpose:
To increase your conscious ability to shift emotional energies from other parts of the body into the heart, where your innate ability to love unconditionally can become increasingly active. And to shift your level of awareness of any particular feeling; to deal with feelings rather than the situations that create them.

Crystal:
In practical terms, whatever crystal is at hand when difficult emotional feelings arise. The crystal is placed on
whatever part of the body is feeling the greatest distress.

Programme:
To shift the energy from the area of body distress into
the heart.

This exercise is to be used when you are experiencing
emotional distress. Lie on the floor or bed, and, with
your eyes closed, scan through your body to identify
where you are feeling the greatest distress. Look for
physical sensations in the body—tension, feelings of
pain or anxiety, some sort of body feeling. When you
have found the area where it feels the worst, place the
crystal directly on that part of the body.

Visualize the crystal 'absorbing' that feeling, and
when there is a sense of transference to the crystal, move
the crystal over your heart. Allow the energy from the
distressed area of your body to flow into your heart. As
that energy floods through your heart, you may well
experience intense emotional release. If there is a feeling
of tightness in the heart or in the throat, do Supplementary Technique 5.

It is important during this exercise to be aware of your
breathing—*don't stop*! You may find that your breathing
rate will increase dramatically, or you may even experience choking or gagging sensations. Don't try to stop or
restrict them. Roll over onto your left side, continue
breathing, and allow your body to release whatever it is
trying to let go of. A box of tissues at hand is not a bad
accompaniment to this exercise.

Several things may happen during this exercise. First,
you may feel a pure sense of transmutation of energy in
the heart—whatever uncomfortable feelings you had
may turn into feelings of joy, of lightness, and you may
experience a warm glow or feeling of heat in the heart.

Alternatively, your Inner Being may choose to release
these energies from the body through some of the
previously described methods—crying, choking or
gagging, or coughing.

In either experience, when you have completed this

exercise and have some sort of release, roll immediately onto your left side, curl up in the foetal position, and allow your breathing to return to normal.

Should images of unpleasant events that created these feelings in the first place arise, take this time of lying on your left side to restructure these events in your own mind, see them as you would have *wished* them to be. In doing so, having released a considerable amount of unharmonious or imbalanced energy, you then feed back into your mind and body positive and loving thoughts, which fill the vacuum left by the release of the previous images.

You may also feel tired and wish to sleep after a deep emotional release, as the muscle tension that has been holding it all in will relax.

As you develop your own heart's capacity to process coarser emotions, you will also develop an increasing capacity to process them as they occur, shifting them in the moment, and empowering yourself to encounter each new experience in an open-hearted way. This does *not* mean that you walk around with your heart open continually, only that your heart is *appropriately* open.

The next exercise is about consciously controlling the openness of your heart, and likewise developing the capacity to close it in appropriate circumstances. It is part of an increasing capacity to choose your own level of experience— to experience things through the coarser emotions (as it is often perfectly appropriate to do), or to shift into the heart, and experience things at that level. You are just as stuck within yourself walking around open-hearted, as you are closed-hearted.

By now, having done the previous exercises in this book, you will have begun to notice specific body sensations around the heart when you are having certain experiences. This exercise is designed to home in on those experiences, and begin to put them under conscious control, self-mastery.

The Lens of the Heart

Purpose:
To be able to open and close the heart at will.

Crystal:
Any crystal you have already been using in connection with your own heart centre.

Programme:
To reflect back to you the body sensations of open-heartedness, and closed-heartedness.

This exercise can be done sitting or lying down, with the crystal placed over the heart.

To begin, think of a time when you felt a feeling of overwhelming love for someone, in other words when your heart was very open. As you think this thought, feel the body feelings that are associated with it, especially those in the heart. More than likely, you will experience a very expansive feeling in the chest, especially a sensation that the chest muscles have relaxed, and that your shoulders have moved back as a result.

Then, remember a time when someone said something very hurtful to you, particularly a person for whom you felt very open-hearted or warm feelings. As you remember this, you will most likely feel a closing sensation in the chest area, as if the chest muscles over the heart have tightened, and you may notice that your shoulders have moved forward. Notice also any other body sensations connected with this.

Go through this cycle a number of times, alternating between open-hearted memories and closed-hearted memories. Each time notice the body response.

When you have done this a few times you will begin to notice which muscles are involved, and where and when they tighten up or relax. Then, practise using your body muscles *without* the invoking memories, placing those muscles under conscious control, to reproduce the same body sensations. As you do this, notice how you feel in your own heart—open or closed. With practice, you can invoke these sensations at will, and, through biofeedback, you can induce 'mood' changes in your own heart just by invoking the body responses.

The final result of this will be an ability to open or close your heart centre at will, and to choose for yourself the state of your own heart as circumstances dictate.

The ability to work directly with your own heart centre will have an enormous impact, both on your health, and on the health of your personal relationships. The most powerful line for me from the Loving Relationships Training was: 'Love brings up anything unlike itself for the purpose of healing.'

This means that you will attract people to you in personal relationships who will trigger in you your own deepest feelings that are *not* love. You are drawn together in your relationship in the first place by love, and your relationship will be maintained by love, but the actual feelings that come boiling to the surface may be anything but! This process usually develops in a new relationship over a period of several months.

It can be quite shocking and dismaying to be in a wonderful new relationship where there are very deep feelings of love and trust, and then all of a sudden, feelings of anger, hatred and resentment came boiling to the surface. You wonder what has gone wrong. In fact, everything is going *exactly right*. You and your partner are healing each other, by bringing anything to the surface that is not love.

By using the techniques of this book, you can begin to shift those feelings into other levels of experience and see them for what they are: a neon arrow pointing directly to the aspects of yourself that are keeping you from inner wholeness.

Inevitably in a truly loving relationship there will be numerous crises. These mostly come about because of our attachment to the belief that other people 'cause' us to have certain feelings. This belief is so deeply imbedded in our culture, and thus in our own psyche, that we will all need a great deal of practice to work through it. Like any other bad habit.

As we gain increased amounts of understanding of ourselves, we also begin to gain increased amounts of understanding into our partners and their processes. This empowers us to work hand in hand with them on their own opening process, as indeed they can work hand in hand with us for ours. The ultimate result will be a healthier body, a healthier mind, and a healthier Being.

It is vitally important to remember that **you chose all of this.**

You chose a set of parents who would fail you in appropriate ways to set up the learning that you have chosen for yourself in this lifetime. This has been repeated several times in this book, but it can't be emphasized strongly enough. Blaming your parents for your failures is keeping you stuck. It is only when you can accept that you chose them for that very purpose, that you can begin to free yourself to be who you really are. Blaming is a form of attachment, and it creates a powerful energetic bond. The tie-cutting exercises in this book are designed to energetically start breaking that bondage. And, when you free yourself, you also free the person that you are blaming.

It is possible through the next exercise to explore exactly *what* you have chosen for this life, and, in the exercise that follows that one, to gain a deeper understanding of *why* you chose it.

Earlier in the book, I talked about the pattern of energy deep in the heart centre, which you will have now explored for yourself at the Sacred Spring. It is this pattern of your Beingness that set up for you the pattern of your own life; to give yourself the experiences necessary for self-completion. Your life purpose is no less than that.

What those patterns are, and the underlying life purpose, is the goal of the following exercise:

Life Purpose

Purpose:
To go back to the moment of your conception, and to see the pattern of your own life.

Crystal:
Choose a crystal for this exercise with the intention of reflecting back to you the pattern of your own life. The crystal is held in the hand for this meditation.

Programme:
To reflect back to you the pattern of your own life as it
will unfold, as seen at the moment of your conception.

This exercise is done sitting, with the crystal held in the
hand. You are going to go backwards in your memory in
stages, until you are back to the exact instant when your
parents' energies connected, and you were conceived.

Begin by going back in your memory to events that
took place a year ago, and feel the feelings and the
thoughts which were happening to you at that time.

Then go back two years from the present and do the
same. Then five years. Then, go backwards in five-year
stages until you reach the age of 15.

Then, begin going back in one- or two-year stages,
and just remember and feel how it was to be 14, and
then 13, and 12, and so forth. As you begin to reach the
earlier years, you will feel your body becoming smaller,
and you will begin to remember your perspective of seeing
the world from the eyes of a child.

Continuing going backward until you reach one year
of age, and continue to go backward in two-month
intervals, until you reach the age of one month. As you
continue to go backwards to the moment of your birth
you will find your body becoming even smaller, and
then you will feel yourself sliding through a dark tunnel,
until you can feel the enclosing walls of the womb
around you.

Again, examine your thoughts and feelings—how was
it just before I was born? What was I thinking and feeling?

Then, continue to go backwards in one-month intervals
while you are inside the womb. You may feel your body
becoming very tiny now, and you may even find the urge
to physically curl up. By all means do so if you feel the
desire. As you come closer and closer to the moment of
conception, you may find yourself floating, awaiting an
energetic connection to be made, like a switch being
thrown. You may experience this energetic connection
as a flash of light—or as a bolt of energy. But, in that
moment of energy connection, you will be able to see
the pattern and purpose of your life as it will unfold.
You will know in that moment the major events and

traumas, some of the people you are going to meet, and some of the lessons you will have to learn. And, you will also have a knowledge of the purpose of your life.

This may not all occur the first time you do this exercise, but continue to repeat it until you have a clear image of what happened in that first moment. You are likely to find answers to many of the mysteries of your own life here.

When you have found what you wish to find, or at least all that is visible in that moment, then allow yourself to return to the womb, and begin to age once again in one-month intervals, noticing at each interval what your thoughts and feelings are, and what your beliefs about life were as they were being formed in the womb. You may make some quite surprising discoveries about some of the ideas and injunctions about your life that came from this time. If there are limiting beliefs that formed here, you can use the tie-cutting exercise later to begin releasing them. Then, when you have reached the time of your birth, see yourself sliding down the tunnel, coming out into the world.

As you do this, you may also be aware of any ideas and beliefs that occurred around the time of your birth, and you can begin working with these through the exercises in this book.

Once you are out of the womb, begin progressing in one-year intervals to the age of 15, and then progress to five-year intervals, noticing along the way life events that have reinforced, or any outworkings of, the life patterns you discovered at the moment of your conception.

When you return to the present, *immediately* sit down with your notebook and note in detail everything you can about this experience. When you repeat this experience later on, do it without reference to your notes. Make a separate set of notes, and see if the two agree. If they do, then you are certain to be getting in close touch with your true life pattern. If not, there may be some illusion slipping in along the way, and you should keep repeating the exercise until you can discover its source.

Having uncovered much of the purpose and pattern of your own life through the previous exercise, the following exercise has been designed to take you into an even larger realm, the realm in which you exist already, but of which you have lost most conscious awareness. It is the place you came from, and it is the place to which you will return.

The Pre-Conception State

Purpose:
To experience that aspect of your Beingness that existed before you were conceived.

Crystal:
For this exercise, use a crystal for the brow and the heart.

Programme:
To reflect back to you the level of your Being that existed prior to your conception.

This exercise is identical to the Life Purpose exercise, except that this time when you come back to the moment of conception, you will feel yourself moving rapidly through another dark tunnel. When you emerge from that tunnel, you will find yourself in a place full of light, and you may well find yourself surrounded by other beings, many of whom you will recognize. When you are in this place, you will be able to remember any conversations that were taking place, and any knowledge that you had about your forthcoming lifetime. While you are in this place you will also be able to understand the reason you have taken on the learning that you have in this lifetime, and what greater purpose it all serves.

When you have learned all that you can learn or wish to learn in this place, then feel yourself sliding down that tunnel at the moment of your conception. Then, follow the same procedure to return back to the present time as in the previous exercise.

What you may discover in this pre-conception place is whether or not you wanted to incarnate (many people didn't), and how you felt about it one way or the other.

As you become more and more aware of your own aspect of choice in coming into life, you will become increasingly aware that all that has happened to you in this life has been your creation and your choosing. Every person who has 'caused' you pain and suffering has been trying to teach you something, and you attracted these people to you for just that purpose.

And the one person you almost always forget to forgive is yourself. Forgive yourself for all of your mistakes, all of your blunders, all of the trouble and pain you have got yourself into. For, from the very deepest level of your being, these are the lessons that you have given yourself. And forgive your body for all of its aches and pains and ills and hurts. Once again, it is only doing these things as part of the teaching you have chosen for yourself.

Many of us carry a deep guilt about wanting to be alive and wanting to have a body, as we believe that in doing so we have separated ourselves from our own Source. For many of us, perhaps for all of us, our experience of having our first body was as if we cut ourselves off from God in order to get it. And, when we began to experience the malfunctions of that body that were trying to teach us, we blamed God for punishing us, believing that He was doing so because we had taken on a body in the first place.

The origins of these sort of beliefs will be talked about in the next chapter, although you may have already begun to discover these things for yourself in the preceding exercises.

Forgiveness

Purpose:
To consciously and deliberately complete the act of forgiveness with any person who has 'caused' you pain and suffering.

Crystal:
A crystal to go over the heart, chosen for a feeling of freshness and newness.

Programme:
To reflect back to you the deepest levels of your own forgiveness, and to reflect back to you your own sense of

completion with people from your past and present.

This exercise is done sitting, with a crystal over the heart. Go into the crystal as in the previous exercises, experiencing your crystal as a crystal room. You will find a chair sitting against one 'wall' of your crystal, for you to sit in. Opposite that chair will be another chair, for the person with whom you wish to have a completion.

There is a door to the right-hand side of the chair sitting opposite, and a door to the left-hand side. The person with whom you wish to complete through forgiveness will enter through the right door, and exit through the left.

Invite each person in turn to come through the door and sit in the chair, and say to each person in turn: 'I understand that what you did was to teach me more about myself, to help me return to my full Humanity. In expressing my forgiveness to you, I release any anger, hatred, resentment, or any other feeling other than love that I have felt for you as a result of our experience together. And, I ask your understanding and forgiveness that I did not understand at the time what you were trying to do.'

You may find other words to use that are equally appropriate for you.

If the person in the opposite chair is someone you have never seen, such as the doctor who delivered you or someone who caused you pain at birth, or is an even more abstract Being such as God, then visualize a person who has an appropriate symbolic form; your perfect image of the word 'doctor', or whatever personification God might take on.

Be aware of your own feelings and responses as you do this exercise. Even if you have feelings for the other person or Being that are not purely love at this point complete the exercise anyway. The act of intention to forgive will set in motion other events and experiences in your life that will lead you to that completion, and don't forget to put yourself in the opposite chair.

When you have completed the experience, allow the crystal to shrink back to its normal size and you return back to yours.

The next chapter deals with past lives, and it is the last chapter for that very reason. Past-life regression is of a certain usefulness in self-discovery, but it only supplements the other techniques of self-discovery that you have been using throughout the book. Its *only* value is as it relates to the life you are living now. If you are not comfortable with the idea of past lives, then you can finish this book with this chapter. If you wish to explore the matter further, then the final chapter will lead you through an exercise in doing just that. The last chapter is oriented around the time of Atlantis, which may or may not have any relevance for you.

Whether or not you become involved with the last chapter, you have had an opportunity through the exercises of the book to this point to look deeply into your own origin, your own Source, which is your own Beingness that resides in your heart. As you go deeper and deeper into your heart, you will come more into contact with your Source. And as you do so, you will discover that you are your own creation.

It is written: In the beginning was the Word. You are your own Word; but the Word must come from the Heart.

8 The Wounded Heart

Throughout this book we have been exploring many aspects of the human heart, and in this chapter, we will look at why you are not already fully the being that you really are.

This chapter is about the time of Atlantis. The whole subject of Atlantis is, from some points of view at least, highly debatable. On a purely scientific basis, there is little or no evidence whatever that Atlantis existed. On the other hand, speaking as a geologist, I can also say the events of Atlantis as remembered by many, and as portrayed in popular literature, are, at least from the geological point of view, not at all impossible.

There may have been, at other times and places, other civilizations on the Earth before Atlantis. But, the Atlantean time seems to be the most relevant one where the human heart is concerned.

The information I will present to you in this chapter is purely my own. My own, in the sense firstly that it is my own personal memory of the time, and, beyond that, it is also compiled from the memories of many hundreds of people that I have worked with in one form or another in the past several years.

These memories come from a wide selection of people, many of which were on no sort of 'spiritual' path whatever.

By far the largest group of memories, well over a hundred, appeared during the hundred-odd courses that I have given on crystals during the past few years, and more recently in courses I have given jointly with colour therapist Lilian Verner-Bonds. Although in our joint course there is a specific process to elicit Atlantis memories (the 'River of Time' process in the next chapter), many of these memories have arisen for the most part, 'spontaneously', just through the simple act of handling the crystals during one of the experiences in the course. This experience is solely oriented toward the participants feeling their own personal reaction to whatever crystal was being held, and absolutely no effort whatever is made to elicit past-life memories. And yet, the memories were appearing anyway. For me, the significance of these memories went beyond the fact that they were appearing at all!

What I began noticing after a while, was that almost all of these memories had several relevant points in common. Not every memory would have all of the points, although some did, but every memory would have two or three at least. And often, these memories would be accompanied by a very strong emotional catharsis, and could, in many instances, be tied directly into current lifetime situations.

One of the most striking and powerful of these situations occurred during a course I was giving in Australia in 1983. I was giving a course to a group of people who had all gone through a particular personal development course not at all related to crystals. This personal development course was highly oriented around the process of catharsis, deep emotional release. At the time, I was most uncomfortable myself with my own deepest feelings, so I made a rule at the beginning of the course: no catharsis!

By the end of the first day, had I been more aware of it at the time, I would have noticed that there was a great deal of fidgeting and general uncomfortable feeling among many of the group participants. I would point out here again, that these people were not of any particular spiritual following, but came from all walks of life—housewives, professional people, working people.

By the next morning, many of these people had deep feelings coming up, and were utterly ready to explode! And they did just that.

About half an hour before the course was to begin, one of the participants went into catharsis at the back of the room, and within five minutes at least 15 people had followed suit. Fortunately, many of the course participants who were not in catharsis had had experience in working with the process, and they were able to aid one another. By the time another 10 or 15 minutes had passed, fully half of the group was experiencing one sort of traumatic release or another coming up around the period of Atlantis, and especially around the use of crystals in Atlantis.

Once again, the major points of memory of that time period were leaping out, but what was so striking for me was that there were several people in the room whose memories interlocked.

There was one particular memory of a man fleeing destruction at the end of Atlantis, and returning to a cave where he had hidden his family away, only to find his daughter dead. On the other side of the room while his memory was happening, was his wife, who, totally unknown to him, was going through the memory of dying in a cave at the end of Atlantis, and, as an out-of-body experience, seeing her father arrive to find her already dead. The other half of exactly the same memory!

Within that same group of people, there was also another interlocking set of memories, but this time with two people who were unknown to each other before the course.

I have also been in numerous self-development courses as a participant, and, once again, I have seen a large number of Atlantean memories 'spontaneously' appear among people who have absolutely no knowledge or interest in this time period, and in courses with utterly no 'spiritual' orientation whatever.

My last source is from my own work as a past-life therapist. Once again, a significant number of memories, again checking out with one another in their main details, often led to major breakthroughs in the personal development of the clients involved, as they were able to see patterns in this lifetime that are just repetitions or a working through of an Atlantis experience.

Above everything else, what has been so clearly underlined for me in each and every one of these experiences, is not so much the experiences themselves, but their effect on the long-term development, usually over many lifetimes, of the people involved.

And in every single instance the area most affected was the human heart. But why the heart centre in particular? As we have seen the heart centre is truly the seat of the Being, and although other energy centres of the body are inevitably affected, the cumulative effect will be most clearly through the heart centre; everything which affects the Being will in some way be reflected through this particular centre. And as the heart centre is the seat and source of love energy, the energy which drives the cosmos, any obstructions to the free flow of energy from this centre ultimately keep us from self-fulfilment, from who we truly are.

In talking about Atlantis, it is important to underline the idea that Atlantis was a *culture*, rather than just thinking of it as a particular place. In the time of Atlantis, a situation existed on the earth not unlike we have today: over a certain part of the earth, a highly developed technological civilization, indeed, a civilization that has flown to the moon, and has reached up to the stars; and yet on another part of the earth, human civilizations that are barely out of the Stone Age.

So how did Atlantis come to be established? Why was it so technologically advanced, when the rest of the earth was literally in the Stone Age?

The answers to these questions may seem absurd to some, or no surprise at all to others. If you find these ideas absurd or offensive, then ignore them. The ideas about, and the techniques of, heart opening in this book work whether you believe any of this or not.

The universe is moving into greater and greater density through the conversion of hydrogen in the stars into denser material, through fusion. As the universe moves into increasingly dense states of being, so therefore must the consciousness of the universe learn to participate in, and live through, its own density. Atlantis was nothing more than that.

Highly evolved beings came to the earth, to learn to inhabit extremely dense bodies.

Atlantis was an experiment. An experiment in dense living.

During the time before the founding of Atlantis, there was a great debate about the suitability of the human body as a vessel for higher consciousness. There were valid arguments on both sides, but the strongest argument against, was that the body itself was too dense. Too dense, at least in the sense of a fear amongst some of the founders that we would lose our fine and subtle connections with our Source through getting too involved with such a heavy level of density. The argument was put forward that an intermediate type of body should be experimented with first, perhaps an amphibian or reptile type of body on another planet with less gravity, and less dense physical bodies. This idea was, ultimately, rejected.

In the long run of things, that argument proved correct. And yet the major argument in favour has *also* proven correct—that the human body is a highly suitable learning instrument. It's just that the lessons we have been learning with it were not necessarily the lessons as originally foreseen!

Atlantis, then, was implanted on the Earth. It is only because of our narrow view of ourselves and our own place in the universe that such an idea may seem startling. I am reminded of a line spoken by an extraterrestrial in a novel by the astronomer Carl Sagan: 'You mustn't think of the universe as a wilderness. It hasn't been for billions of years. Think of it more as . . . cultivated.'

There are certainly other experiments in dense living going on elsewhere in the universe, but one thing which makes the Atlantean civilization unique is that it failed.

Mention is made in various writings and teachings about civilizations which existed prior to Atlantis on the earth—Lemuria and Mu. I have no personal knowledge of these civilizations, and they have yet to emerge in one single instance from any of the past-life experiences I have talked about previously. In any event, the only civilization on the earth that seems to be having any effect in this current life-time, is that of Atlantis.

Almost all memories place the time of Atlantis between 12 and 15,000 years ago. Several people have recalled having several lives in Atlantis, although the usual experience is that only one of those lifetimes, normally the last one, is still creating effects today. The whole time around the ending of Atlantis was deeply traumatic for everyone who was involved, and the failure of such a massive undertaking left virtually no one untouched.

I have already said that Atlantis was an experiment in living in dense matter, but there was a great deal more to it than that. As I have discussed in my other books, there are certain fundamental laws of energy which govern the universe, and the most basic is that energy always balances. In order to balance itself, it effectively moves in a circle. It is a restatement of Isaac Newton's Law: 'For every action, there is an equal and opposite reaction.'

Because everything in the universe is made from energy, everything in the universe must obey this basic law within its own level of being.

As an emergence of this basic balance, comes the law of polarity. Polarity comes from the extremes that are always in a state of tension, in order to come into this state of balance. And it is this tension of polarities that creates the energy for growth.

So, in Atlantis we were here for *experience*. But whatever experience is, experience must also be an energy, because *everything* is. So, this can also be drawn as a circle of energy:

As you experience something

something experiences you

Thus, as you experience something, that 'thing' also experiences you. In the case of Atlantis, we were there to experience the earth, but likewise the earth was also experiencing us; the polarity is of student and teacher.

But, as I have often pointed out in courses, if energy truly moves in a circle, then where does one polarity begin and the next one end? There is an old spiritual law which says: 'When the student is ready, the teacher appears.' To which I add: 'The problem is telling who is who!'

Student

Teacher

In the founding of Atlantis, we had this basic understanding of the law of energy in relationship to experience, so one of the focuses of Atlantis was not only to learn *from* the earth but it was very clearly to *teach* the earth. But, what were we teaching here?

Teach the earth

Learn from the earth

Everything in the universe learns through experience, and the earth is no exception. It may seem a bit odd to think of a planet learning, but that comes from only relating to our own human experience of learning. Learning is nothing more than an experience which changes one's perception. So, how is it that a planet can perceive?

The earth is 99.999 per cent minerals, so therefore almost all of its learning must take place at the mineral level of consciousness. It will be a difficult idea for some that minerals have any consciousness whatever, but we need to remember that the universe itself is nothing more than a vast field of consciousness, and that that consciousness penetrates and permeates everything that exists within the universe, including its minerals.

And yes, it is consciousness at a very low level. But, because so much of the material universe exists at a mineral level of Being at this particular time, much of the consciousness of the universe still exists at a mineral level.

The ultimate goal of learning of any sort is expanded consciousness; so therefore learning at a mineral level of Being will ultimately expand the consciousness of that Being. Because the Beings (us) who founded Atlantis were of a very evolved consciousness, this was the earth's experience of us. The experience, through its mineral level of Being, of higher consciousness raises its own consciousness—the consciousness of the mineral level itself!

Because minerals form a set of very distinct and unique patterns, they have a high degree of *resonance* with each other, and therefore in a sense could be said to 'communicate' quite readily with one another. I am obviously not speaking of a verbal communication, but rather communication at an energetic level, a setting up of vibrations that cause a sympathetic vibration in other minerals of a like nature. This also happens at all of the other levels of consciousness as well, and is the underlying basis for the universal law 'like attracts like'. Another way of stating this law is that 'like *resonates* with like'. So, in Atlantis we deliberately set out to be teachers of the earth, to pour into the earth our own higher consciousness. And because the earth exists mainly at a mineral level of being, it was through the earth's minerals, and in particular crystals, that we began to communicate with the earth.

This was the initial use of crystals in Atlantis—crystals that resonated with the earth's crystals and minerals. These crystals were placed at critical points on the earth's surface, points where the earth's own natural lines of energy were focused. These links are often referred to as ley lines. These lines of energy flow are very much like the energy meridians of the human body, and serve essentially the same function within the body of the earth—to keep its energies in a state of balance. And, as with the meridians of the human body, there are certain critical crossing or intersecting points through which a great deal of the body can be influenced by the application of pressure or pins at that critical point, as in accupressure or accupuncture. In the case of the earth, the 'pins' were crystals.

A pin is a tiny object relative to the size of the human body, and yet applied at a critical energy point can create effects throughout much of the body. Likewise, a crystal is relatively small compared to the size of the earth (although these were not small crystals as we usually use the term!), and yet, placed at critical points, crystals were able to begin affecting, through resonance, a great deal of the earth which was connected energetically to those particular points.

These crystals were placed where higher consciousness could be consciously and deliberately poured into them, the so-called 'temples'. They were temples not in the sense of worship, but in the sense of consciously and deliberately making contact with the Beingness of the earth, and attempting, through the crystals, to educate the earth in the higher aspects of love, wisdom, and so forth. And it went well enough for a while. . . .

That Atlantis failed, there is no question. Why it failed, and what could have been done to prevent that failure, has been a source of anguish, guilt and confusion to many people who have now begun to remember their own part in Atlantis. Of all of the accumulated information I have seen over the past several years, I personally come to only one conclusion: *nothing* could have been done to prevent the failure of Atlantis.

Because the Atlantean experience, that of living on a planet of great density, was a new experience for all participants, problems which arose could not have been anticipated. Some of those problems, in fact the majority of them, revolved around the human body. As I mentioned earlier, those who objected to coming to the earth on the basis of the body being too dense, were right. And it is also true that this body is a highly suitable instrument of learning. But, as it turned out, the body turned out to be a bit *too* good.

Living in more subtle levels of energy there is not so much difference between the various levels of energy of your Being, but, with a physical body that has fully descended into matter, the difference between the energy levels at the most subtle level, the soul level, and the physical level, are immense. The major experience that this has is the illusion of separation. By focusing almost purely on the physical, it is very easy to not notice the much more subtle levels. And particularly, as we levels. And particularly, as we got more and more involved got more and more involved with the experience of living in dense matter, it was natural that this is exactly what we did.

At the physical level of Being, it is also possible to create other separations. And I use the word create deliberately, as separation *must be created*. Truly, it is impossible to create separation anyway, because unity is all that exists in the universe. None the less, the illusions that can be created have very powerful effects, especially in the physical or near physical level of Being. And one thing which we appeared to separate ourselves from was our Inner Being, our true Self, our Source.

Not that this was a deliberate choice. But as we began to focus more and more on the physical level of Being, it was almost a matter of 'forgetting'. And because the attraction of living in matter was so great, the seductiveness of the experience led us further and further away from our inner connection to who we really are.

I believe that the inner Being has three major aspects: love, wisdom, and power. These three aspects can be drawn as the corner of a triangle. When these three aspects are in their right relationship, in equal measure, then the sides of the triangle are equal; however if one aspect gets out of balance, is underdeveloped, then one or more sides of the triangle get very narrow, and rather than being a solid structure, the balance of the triangle becomes very easily tipped.

The side of the triangle that became overbalanced in Atlantis was the power aspect. There is nothing wrong with power—it is just that we have mostly experienced it in its unbalanced form, that of manipulation. Indeed, you couldn't walk across a room without the power of your muscles.

But, as with the other two aspects, power by itself, and used by itself, creates an enormous imbalance. You can probably think of a number of examples of people who use power, but without any aspects of love and wisdom. The television character 'JR' is a classic example of this type of personality.

Also, the love aspect can be separated out, and it too can become out of balance. The Flower Power people of the sixties were the classic example of this. Just oozing love, but without the wisdom to use that love in a constructive way, and without the power to accomplish anything even if they had the wisdom.

And the wisdom aspect—the guru on the mountain top.

Full of the wisdom of the ages but without the love to take that wisdom down into the marketplace.

So, we began to focus purely on the aspect of power in Atlantis. We all know how seductive power can be. You have seen it yourself in those around you—at work, at the office, in organizations or groups which you belong to. One small step up the ladder, and the person involved goes berserk. Goes mad with power! And think of the possibilities, if, through the major crystals, you had an entire planet at your mercy.

This is precisely the situation that faced those in the greatest positions of power in Atlantis. Is it any wonder that they succumbed to the temptation? And mostly through lack of experience this was not anticipated.

Through our lack of experience of this level of density, we began to manipulate, we began to exercise our power in ways that were not in keeping with the nature of things. Because time, for example, is less important or totally non-existent at more subtle levels of Being, we began to apply that understanding of time to this level of density where time *is* important. It is not in the nature of things to plant a crop on Wednesday and harvest it on Thursday. And yet, when events did not progress rapidly, we began to manipulate matter, and the aspect of time, by using the power available to us through our links to the earth.

Another error was in the choice of the crystals that were used to work with the earth directly. These crystals were brought to the earth, and were not *of* the earth. Therefore, they lacked a certain natural affinity to the planet, and there was a level of detachment in their use from what was actually being created in the earth.

But the problem most directly related to our own heart centres, was our lack of understanding of our own bodies. To a large degree, we were so arrogant in our surety of our place in the universe, that we could not imagine anything going wrong. And when something did, we began to believe that there was something wrong with the body itself.

Many of you will have memories of 'healing' temples in Atlantis, temples for healing the physical body. Or, you may have read about them; there is a lot of 'channelled' material available about these temples, and about the processes and techniques that were used in them.

But no one has ever asked: why did we *need* healing in Atlantis?

If our physical body is a reflection of our Inner Being, and the founders of Atlantis were very advanced Beings (we are probably talking about you by the way), then what in the world did they need healing for? Why was there illness in Atlantis, if the founders of Atlantis were such highly tuned beings?

The answer was simple. We were starting to slip. We were starting to lose that inner connection. Our bodies were starting to tell us that, saying to us that we were not keeping in harmony with who we really were.

We didn't know that at the time, so when it started to go wrong, we blamed the body. Not unlike medicine today: if something goes wrong, it's the body's fault. All the body was doing was exactly what it was designed to do: to reflect back to us the state of our inner harmony. And in doing 'healing' in Atlantis, all we were really doing was using crystals to manipulate the body back into wellness, purely relieving its symptoms. This is no different than what medicine and indeed many alternative therapies are doing today—manipulating the body to rid it of its symptoms. But in no way touching the disharmony in the inner beliefs that create the illness in the first place.

Many of the horrific manipulations of one another that were going on toward the end of Atlantis had their origin in this time of 'healing' the body.

I won't bother to list all of the various deeds and devices that have turned up in past-life memories, but rather will suffice with a few examples. One of the 'healing' devices that was constructed using crystals was a harness-like device with crystals either over or implanted in various of the chakra centres. This device was originally intended to help harmonize and balance energies, and inevitably involved the heart centre, as that was the area from which our inner Source was being blocked. It was then discovered that these devices could also be used to manipulate body energies, and used to control and manipulate each other.

Likewise, memories have come up of using laser-like crystals as weapons, using them to burn someone down, just through the power of thought. Memories have also come up of using large crystals to suck the life force out of one another.

In each of these examples, there was absolutely nothing wrong with the crystals themselves; they were merely being used as tools and devices, through the conscious effort of their users. But, how had our consciousness managed to slip to the point that we were doing such things?

As I mentioned earlier, this was a result of our focusing purely on the aspect of power, and losing our inner connection with our own aspects of love and wisdom. And because we were doing such things, although we were blocking out awareness of what we were doing through our conscious mind, our unconscious mind was still recording and responding to the horror of what was occurring. This is why there was so much armouring of the heart centre that went on at that time—it was the only way we could survive at a deeper level.

Beyond a certain point the inner disharmony, the loss of connection to the Inner Being throughout the civilization as a whole, became irreversible. The balance was tipped.

This was when the decision was made to end the experiment.

We were in a situation in Atlantis that was a great deal more serious than just a few million people on the earth being involved.

Because of the precisely patterned nature of crystals, they are powerfully connected to one another through resonance. One of the problems in Atlantis was that the crystals brought to the earth were not resonating perfectly with the crystals of the earth.

And, because all things in the universe are connected at a subtle level, resonances set up on the earth are broadcast far, far beyond the earth, thus, the mess we were creating energetically in Atlantis was not just a local problem. Every crystal in use on the earth was resonating with every other crystal like itself *all over the universe*.

So, the decision was made to end Atlantis. Atlantis didn't just give a great sigh and sink beneath the waves. Atlantis was destroyed.

Once again, mistakes were made. Because we had no experience of a civilization like Atlantis going wrong, we also had no experience of ending such a civilization. Thus, a great deal of the destructiveness at the end was unnecessary, but, once again under the circumstances, perhaps unavoidable.

There are many people today who are carrying an enormous amount of grief and guilt about the ending of Atlantis, and many people actually believe that they were personally responsible for its destruction. To a highly limited extent this is true—*every* person who was involved in the ending of Atlantis *was* personally responsible. But, only personally responsible for their part in it, and there were many thousands of individuals involved.

There is likewise a lot of deeply buried grief and guilt about those who were doing the manipulation, and indeed among those who were manipulated.

All of us are setting up life situations to begin working through all of our deepest inner feelings—to remove the energetic blocks that keep us from inner connectedness to our source.

It is important to remember, above all, that Atlantis was just a learning situation. That nothing irreversible has happened, and that all we have done is failed to learn a certain group of lessons. We made some mistakes.

I like to break the word mistake down into two words: mis—take. In filming, if you mess up the first take, you just take another take! Likewise, where the lessons of Atlantis are concerned, we are just taking another take.

I would like to mention the word *karma* at this point. The old and limited view of karma is 'An eye for an eye and a tooth for a tooth.' Karma is really nothing more than a series of unfinished lessons. If you have been in a particular learning situation with someone, and neither of you learned the lesson, it's possible that you will draw that same person back to you in another lifetime to participate in some event or series of events that will recreate the lesson, from the point where you left off. It doesn't have to be the same event. It is the *lesson* that is important, and not the events that create the lesson.

A few years ago, I was absolutely horrified to realize that in the world today we are recreating Atlantis! After a while, I realized that we *have* to. We have to go back to the point where we didn't learn the lesson, where we made the mistakes. You can only begin where you left off.

Another way of thinking of karma is: 'You have to clean up your own mess.' What we have been doing in the time since Atlantis is energetically cleaning up the messes we created through our misuse of power. In the time since we have all had our opportunity to be kings and princes and rulers, persons who exercised a great deal of power. We have been, I hope, learning the lessons of the exercise of power.

So, we get to do it all over again—or not.

Atlantis was not a tragedy; it was a mistake. I often say that you learn to ride a bicycle mostly by falling off a bicycle. When you fall off, you just get back on and try again. So in Atlantis, we just fell off our bicycle!

At least, as we recreate the Atlantean situation this time, we have a great deal of experience, and the enormous number of us who are deeply in touch with our Atlantean experience in our hearts have a resolve to never make that mistake again.

You are making a choice about this matter right now—you have been led to read this book, as indeed I have been led to write it.

Through my own experience of awakening over the past few years, I have had the opportunity to look deep into my own heart, and have come to realize that the *only* way which we will prevent another Atlantis from happening, is to be fully open in our hearts, and always acting from the heart.

In Atlantis, we got into our heads. We closed our hearts to what was going on around us. To a degree, I see this beginning to happen once again with the use of crystals. People have begun, in some instances, to view them as 'gadgets'. It is a head-centred view. When we listen to our hearts, when we listen to the very Source of our own Being, we will never put a foot wrong.

This time, we can get it right.

The River of Time

Purpose:
This exercise can be used for exploring any past life, however in this particular exercise we will especially explore Atlantis. This or any other past life exercise should always be connected to the events of this lifetime to see the outworkings of those lives in the *now*.

As mentioned, I have been a past-life therapist, and have seen so many of the pitfalls of the work. I have fallen into a few of them myself!

The biggest single pitfall is to *identify* with any of your past lives. You may well have been the Queen of Sheba or whoever, *but you are not her now*. You are whoever you are, with *this* personality, in *this* lifetime. What you have now is what you are meant to be dealing with, and past lives are valuable only in the context of what is happening in your life now. That is why in the meditation that follows, a direct connection will be made between then and now.

Crystal:
In choosing a crystal for this exercise, let your intuition guide you to one that 'feels' as if it is connected to Atlantis. It's unnecessary for you to have had any previous memories of this time—just go with the feeling. In choosing crystals to go back to other lifetimes you can use a general intention to choose a crystal that is relevant to a lifetime connected to a particular experience in this lifetime that you are seeking to explore.

Programme:
The specific programme for this crystal is to reflect back to you patterns that originated in Atlantis and have generated events in this lifetime. In programming crystals for other lifetimes, or to seek the underlying patterns of other life events, use a programme that is specific to the particular time or event you are seeking. Or, if that is not clear to you in a moment, use a 'searching' programme, in which you would be looking for *any* reflection from a past lifetime that is relevant to the outworking of your life at the moment.

To begin this exercise visualize going somewhere out of doors, a place you would be happy and comfortable to return to. You will find yourself on the brow of a hill, with a gentle slope running down to a river below you. Fill in the details of the day—the smell of the flowers, the wind in the trees, the sound of birds. And when the image is clear in your mind, walk down the gentle slope to the river, where you will hear the gurgle of the water, the smell of the river itself, and whatever other details about the river you wish to add. This is a gentle and peaceful river and along the bank you will find a boat tied.

This is a unique river, for it is a river of time, and, you will find that this river flows backwards in time.

So, when you are ready, climb into the boat, cast it
loose from the bank, and allow yourself to drift gently
down the river.

As you float down the river, you will see people standing along the bank at various intervals, people that you
have been in other times. In the beginning, you may see
yourself standing on the bank as a young adult, and then
later as a child, and then even further as an infant sitting
on the bank watching you float past.

And as you float further backwards on the river you
will begin to see other people along the bank, people in
other costumes, and perhaps even of a different sex than
you are now. These are all people that you have been in
other lifetimes, and you can float back down this river
any time you wish to explore any of those lifetimes. But
for the moment, we are going a long, long way back in
time—back to Atlantis.

As you float further down the river, you will begin to
notice a certain feeling coming from the crystal that you
are holding for this meditation. It is a feeling that will
somehow correspond to a feeling you had in Atlantis
and as the feeling from the crystal begins to match the
feeling that surrounds you in the river, you will see a
person standing on the riverbank. This is the person
who you were at that time, and that person will serve as
your guide to explore the relevant portions of that lifetime. When you see that person, bring your boat to the
bank, and step out and join your guide on the bank.

Your guide will then lead you along a pathway up the
riverbank, a riverbank just high enough that you will not
be able to see over it as you step from the boat.

You will then climb to the top of the riverbank, and
you will see unfold in front of you a time and place in
Atlantis.

This will be a place that was important to you then, a
place connected to whatever lessons and events are
being created in this lifetime. Your guide will show you
through that time and place—its buildings, costumes,
places that were important to you at that time. And, as
you walk along the pathway, you may well see and meet
people who were important to you, and you may recognize some of them as being important to you in this lifetime.

Your guide will then take you to a certain place, a very specific place where the events happened which generated the patterns that you are working through in this life. Your guide will then leave you standing or sitting in a safe place, where you can watch him act out the events as an observer. For the purposes of this meditation, it will be events connected with your heart centre that are still influencing you in this lifetime.

So, your guide may be joined by others, and they will then act out for you those events. Give yourself a few minutes for all of this to take place. You may see it as one event, or it may be a whole series of events. You may feel the feelings that your guide was feeling, experience those experiences, and feel the deep inner connection of those events to this lifetime.

When your guide has finished acting out those events, should the guide have died in the process, or his or her body become injured or maimed, then take a moment from your place of observation to reach out and heal your guide. If life has departed from that body, then see the life return; if the body has been injured see those injuries heal over, and see that body come back into wholeness and wellness.

Your guide will then join you, and will lead you along the pathway back to the river. If there is anything you don't understand about how those events which your guide has acted out have influenced you in this lifetime, your gentle stroll back to the river is the time to have a chat, and your guide can explain things to you as is necessary.

As you come back over the hill and down to the river, you will notice the river is now flowing forward in time, even though your boat is where you left it. Bid goodbye to your guide, climb into the boat, and cast it loose from the bank once again.

As you float back forward in time, as you drift along, you may wish to see standing along the bank other people that you have been in other lifetimes—other lifetimes where you have been working through and working out the patterns which began in Atlantis.

Just make a note of who those people were for the moment, and you can come back and explore those lifetimes with those people as your guide at any time. But for now, return to your starting place and, when you come out of your meditation, pick up your notebook and pen and record as many details as you can remember.

As you explore this and other past lives, you will begin to see the patterns of this life more clearly, the patterns you have been unravelling throughout this book.

And therein, find, at a deeper level, the Being that you really are, and bring that Being into fuller and fuller manifestation.

And as you do so, become more fully and richly Human.

It is a journey to the Heart.

References

Piero Ferrucci, *What We May Be* (Los Angeles, Jeremy P. Tarcher Inc., 1982).

Michael Gauquelin, *The Cosmic Clocks* (London, Peter Owen, 1967).

John Harrison, *Love Your Disease* (London, Angus & Robertson, 1984).

Alexander Lowen, *Bioenergetics* (London, Penguin, 1975).

——*Pleasure* (out of print, publisher not known).

Desmond Morris, *The Naked Ape* (London, Corgi, 1967).

Richard Moss, *The I That Is We* (Berkeley Celestial Arts, 1981).

Dorothy Retallack, *The Sound of Music and Plants* (Santa Monica, DeVorss & Co., 1973).

John Whitman, *The Psychic Power of Plants* (London, Star Books, 1974).

Additional Readings

In addition to the books listed above, I also recommend:

Bob Mandel and Sondra Ray, *Birth and Relationships*, (Berkeley, California, Celestial Arts, 1987).

Robin Norwood, *Women Who Love too Much*, (New York, Pocket Books, 1985).

Sondra Ray, *Loving Relationships*, (Berkeley, California, Celestial Arts, 1980).

Gail Sheehy, *Passages*, (London, Bantam, 1974).

——*Pathfinders*, (London, Bantam, 1985).

Lewis Thomas, *The Lives of a Cell*, (London, Bantam, 1984).

Dr Thomas Verny, *The Secret Life of the Unborn Child*, (London, Sphere, 1982).

Index

Of further interest . . .

COSMIC CRYSTALS

Crystal Consciousness and the New Age

Ra Bonewitz

This absorbing and best-selling book reveals the hidden world of crystals: their formation, properties and their key role in the Age of Rebirth we are now experiencing – the Age of Aquarius.
COSMIC CRYSTALS describes:
- healing and meditation with crystals
- crystals and planetary healing
- crystal dowsing
- energy effects of crystals
- growing your own crystals